Praise for

THE LEADER ASSISTANT

Jeremy's book infuses assistants with a blend of practical expertise and insightful wisdom that inspires confidence, promotes leadership, and increases enthusiasm for this essential role.

—PEGGY GRANDE, FORMER EXECUTIVE ASSISTANT
TO PRESIDENT RONALD REAGAN

In a clear and compelling style, Jeremy offers relevant, up-to-the-minute nuts-and-bolts advice for assistants at every level. He is a refreshing and important voice in the administrative professional landscape. If you're serious about working as a true business partner, this book is required reading.

—BONNIE LOW-KRAMEN, THOUGHT LEADER AND
AUTHOR OF *BE THE ULTIMATE ASSISTANT*

Jeremy is thoughtful, thought-provoking, and he's walked a mile in my shoes. If you want to be a better assistant, read this book!

—MELINDA VAIL-GOODNIGHT, EXECUTIVE
ASSISTANT, SOUTHWEST AIRLINES

He's the best daddy ever!

—WESTON AND SILAS BURROWS, SONS OF THE
AUTHOR, EXPERT LEGO BUILDERS

Jeremy is blazing new ground. This concept of the Leader Assistant is woefully understudied. Jeremy is methodically leading the exploration of one of the most potent active ingredients in organizations today. I urge you to embrace his important redefinition of the executive assistant.

—LARRY ZARIN, RETIRED SVP AND CHIEF
MARKETING OFFICER, EXPRESS SCRIPTS

Jeremy's book is full of actionable, practical advice, and it reads as if he's sitting in the room having a conversation with you. The Leader Assistant is a must-read for any assistant looking to level up, as well as any CEO looking to create a more productive working relationship with their assistant.

—JESS LINDGREN, HOST OF THE *ASK AN ASSISTANT*
PODCAST AND EA TO PAT FLYNN, HOST OF
THE SMART PASSIVE INCOME PODCAST

This. Book. Is. Spot. On. Jeremy is the real deal—he was "walking his walk" way before he ever thought about "talking his talk." I'm not sure there is someone on this planet who not only better understands the role and best practices for being a Leader Assistant, but can articulate the hows, whys, dos, and don'ts so effectively.

—MIKE WEINBERG, BESTSELLING AUTHOR AND SPEAKER

Reading this book is like having a cup of coffee with Jeremy, a master executive assistant. He gives you all the coaching you need to learn how to master your craft as an assistant.

—GINA COTNER, FOUNDER AND CEO,
ATHENA EXECUTIVE SERVICES

My time as a C-suite executive assistant and chief of staff at some of the largest tech companies in the world taught me one thing:

Everyone, myself included, has room to improve their leadership skills. Whether you're a part-time remote virtual assistant or the chief of staff at a billion-dollar company, this book will help you LEAD.

—AL-HUSEIN N. MADHANY, FOUNDING PARTNER OF
TACK ADVISORS AND ASSISTANTSGUIDE.COM

With engaging stories, real-time examples from the field, and Jeremy's trademark direct approach, this book deserves to be on the professional-development bookshelf of every career admin.

—LUCY BRAZIER, CEO OF MARCHAM PUBLISHING,
PUBLISHERS OF *EXECUTIVE SECRETARY MAGAZINE*

Jeremy clearly outlines what it takes to be a Leader Assistant in a practical and challenging way. If you're an assistant, or if you have an assistant, read this book.

—JOHN RUHLIN, CEO AND AUTHOR OF *GIFTOLOGY*

Jeremy has created a relevant, easy-to-read field guide for any assistant who wants to step into leadership and become a game-changing assistant.

—JULIE PERRINE, FOUNDER AND CEO OF ALL THINGS
ADMIN, AUTHOR OF *THE INNOVATIVE ADMIN*™

I have a rising optimism for the career executive assistant when I consider the relevance and strategic importance of this profession, wherein opportunities abound. In The Leader Assistant, Jeremy masterfully elevates this role and places it in a realm of well-deserved achievement. This book is a must-read for those who wish to gain a deeper understanding of the vitality and profound impact of this career in our global workplace.

—MELBA J. DUNCAN, PRESIDENT, THE DUNCAN GROUP,
INC., AND CEO, DUNCAN LEADERSHIP INSTITUTE

I've had the opportunity to work alongside some world-class assistants over the course of my businesses. Somehow, they intuitively knew what is now listed and described in this book for you. Take what's in this book and use it! Trust me, it will pay off in great ways for your time and results.

—BRYAN MILES, CHAIRMAN AND CO-FOUNDER OF BELAY

Jeremy provides real strategies that assistants can implement into their work, which will make them more efficient and effective.

—NICKY CHRISTMAS, FOUNDER AND EDITOR
OF PRACTICALLY PERFECT PA

I've known Jeremy since he was twelve. He used to ask me (his youth pastor at the time) where we were going next and what our plan was. Fifteen years later, Jeremy was my executive assistant, and I looked to him for guidance. He helped me maximize my influence as a leader. Assistants, this book is the guide to transform your career.

—DARRIN PATRICK, AUTHOR, SPEAKER, AND PASTOR

Jeremy's passion and wisdom are coupled with honesty, purpose, and integrity. He understands firsthand what it takes to be an exceptional Leader Assistant. Jeremy is brilliant at sharing his experiences to guide others. I am honored and privileged to know him and be part of his community.

—JILLIAN HUFNAGEL, EXECUTIVE COACH,
FACILITATOR, AND STRATEGIST

Jeremy's book is the essential guide for assistants who want to grow their confidence, anticipate the needs of their executive, and embrace the calling of a leader.

—PAIGE MCPHEELY, CEO OF BASE (SOFTWARE FOR EAS)

I LOVE this book! As a career executive (Leader) Assistant turned CEO, I wish I would've had this book at the beginning of my career. It's the perfect reference guide for new and established assistants, and provides the perfect roadmap and aha moments that create the mindset, practices, and follow-through necessary to be a highly competent Leader Assistant. Kudos to Jeremy for capturing the ever-changing nuance of this role in no uncertain terms. This is THE book for EAs to keep within reach throughout their careers.

—PHOENIX NORMAND, AUTHOR, CHIEF OF TRĪB

Jeremy is a fierce advocate for the assistant community and has distilled his knowledge of what it takes to be a game-changing assistant into practical and actionable steps. The new assistant is rewriting history, and Jeremy is leading the charge.

—HALLIE WARNER, CHIEF OF STAFF, ADAM HERGENROTHER COMPANIES

I was lucky enough to work with Jeremy, EA-to-EA, in my last role, and it's wonderful to see him sharing his expertise. I found myself nodding my head in agreement so many times while reading this book. I wouldn't hesitate to recommend that every EA read this (and keep it on the desk for quick reference and encouragement)!

—CRYSTAL ESQUIVEL, FORMER EA, NOW CHIEF OF STAFF AT BASE (SOFTWARE FOR EAS)

Jeremy's reach and generous commitment to the EA community spans the globe through his podcast, blog, social platforms, and now his first book. Thank you, Jeremy, for shining a light on the value we bring to our executives and our orgs.

—MAGGIE JACOBS, AUTHOR AND EXECUTIVE ADMINISTRATOR

The Leader Assistant isn't just a "how-to" book for assistants and executives. It's a powerful tool full of examples, templates, stories, and insights that are relevant for assistants at every level.

—LINDA MCFARLAND, AUTHOR OF *THE WIZARD BEHIND THE CEO* AND *SITTING ON A FILE CABINET, NAKED, WITH A GUN*, AND EXPERIENCED C-LEVEL EXECUTIVE ASSISTANT IN SILICON VALLEY

Jeremy touches on all the issues assistants need to become a game changer. His experience is more than visible. He knows what he's talking about, which makes the book so special.

—DIANA BRANDL, FOUNDER OF *THE FUTURE ASSISTANT PODCAST* AND THE SOCIALISTA PROJECTS

This is a must-read book for any assistant who wants to self-lead. It is packed with sound advice and uncovers many areas assistants might not consider but are important.

—JOAN BURGE, FOUNDER AND CEO, OFFICE DYNAMICS INTERNATIONAL

A game-changing assistant is someone who knows what to do, when to do it, and how to do it. We all know it's anything but easy, but if you follow the steps Jeremy has skillfully laid out in this guide, you will be a game-changing assistant!

—RHONDA SCHARF, HALL OF FAME SPEAKER, AUTHOR, CONSULTANT, AND PRODUCER OF #ADMINSROCK CONFERENCE

Jeremy offers timely, relevant, and insightful guidance for assistants who strive to be leaders in their industry. An easy and enjoyable read, he captures the perfect blend of practical insights and personal stories.

—ANNIE CRONER, EXECUTIVE PERSONAL ASSISTANT AND FOUNDER OF WHOLEASSISTANT.COM

THE
LEADER
ASSISTANT

*Four Pillars of a **Confident**,*
***Game-Changing** Assistant*

JEREMY BURROWS

THE LEADER ASSISTANT
Four Pillars of a Confident, Game-Changing Assistant

ISBN   978-1-5445-0946-4   *Hardcover*
   978-1-5445-0945-7   *Paperback*
   978-1-5445-0944-0   *Ebook*

Bio Headshot by Erica Karleskint

To my Grandpa, Harold.

You were a hard-working entrepreneur who rested well.

Thank you for showing me what humble confidence looks like.

To my Grandma, Lorene.

Several years into my assistant career, I discovered you'd been an assistant to a top executive at Trans World Airlines. It was then I knew where my passion for the administrative profession came from.

Thank you for showing me how to lead through simple things like to-do lists, kindness, and punctuality.

I miss you and I can't wait to exchange assistant stories with you.

CONTENTS

———

FOREWORD 13

INTRODUCTION 17

PROLOGUE 23

PILLAR 1: EMBODY THE CHARACTERISTICS

1. THE ESSENTIAL CHARACTERISTICS 31

2. THE GAME-CHANGING CHARACTERISTICS 43

3. DISCERNING 49

4. STEADY 55

5. CONFIDENT 63

6. HUMBLE 71

7. FUTURE-PROOF 77

PILLAR 2: EMPLOY THE TACTICS

8. TIME MANAGEMENT 91

9. TASK AND INTERRUPTION MANAGEMENT 95

10. CALENDAR 107

11. MEETINGS 117

12. EMAIL 129

13. TRAVEL 139

14. PROFESSIONAL DEVELOPMENT 143

15. GOALS 151

16. NEGOTIATION 159

17. THE PERFECT RESUME 165

18. COMMUNICATION 171

PILLAR 3: ENGAGE IN RELATIONSHIPS

19. THE DEHUMANIZATION OF ASSISTANTS 181

20. NETWORKING 187

21. YOUR EXECUTIVE 195

22. YOUR COWORKERS 211

PILLAR 4: EXERCISE SELF-CARE

23. BURNOUT CREEP 221

24. BURNOUT STRESSORS AND SIGNS 225

25. FIVE ANTIDOTES TO BURNOUT 233

CONCLUSION 243

RESOURCES 245

ACKNOWLEDGMENTS 247

ABOUT THE AUTHOR 251

FOREWORD

ARE YOU READY TO LEAD?

BY MONIQUE HELSTROM

I had the advantage of learning from the foremost leadership expert, Simon Sinek, as I was his "Chief of Simon" for nearly a decade. During that time, one of the most essential lessons I learned is that leadership and rank are not the same thing. I've met plenty of those who sit at the top of organizations and command authority, and we do as we are told because of that authority, but they are not *leaders*. I have also met many working in the middle or bottom ranks of organizations, and they absolutely are *leaders*.

This is because leadership is not about power, title, or salary. Leadership is an act, a practice, a discipline to take care of the people around us, regardless of how the team, client, or executive is showing up. It's how *we* make the world a better place for the person to our right and the person to our left. Leadership is about strength, integrity, gratitude, fortitude, patience, empathy, and generosity.

You, too, can be a *leader*, and the world needs you to act as such.

Make no mistake, you carry a heavy load. You are expected to have a high leadership capacity and to "make things happen"— even when your colleagues fail to lead, support, or get out of your way. You are expected to think ahead, communicate up, look down, and stay balanced. You are expected to be the backbone, the innovator, the task-doer, the culture-keeper, the encyclopedia, the workaholic, and about a thousand more... and are expected to do so with a wink and a smile. This is the hard truth.

And within that lies the power of choice. You can choose to play the victim and let the heavy load wear you down until your relationships and health are at risk. Or you can choose to change the script—right here and right now.

CHOOSE TO BE THE LEADER YOU WISH YOU HAD. Know in your heart that you help those around you accomplish their mission, that you are valuable, and that you help businesses succeed. You have more strength and resourcefulness than most, and you never back down from a challenge. And when you finally make the choice to lead with passion, to keep a positive outlook, and to hold your head up high with pride, the entire assistant profession rises with you.

Continue to lead by serving those around you. Look for opportunities to fill the leadership gaps in your workplace. Use your voice. You have an opportunity not only to make your organization better, but to make the world better.

People look to you—the assistant—for guidance and leadership.

Are you ready to lead?

—Monique Helstrom
Founder, On Point
Former Executive Assistant and Chief of Simon Sinek
MoniqueHelstrom.com

INTRODUCTION

HOW TO USE THIS BOOK

I still have a handwritten note from leadership guru and bestselling author John Maxwell. I met him when I was nine and asked him to sign a copy of his book, *Leadership 101: Inspirational Quotes & Insights for Leaders.*

His note read:

> "Jeremy, you're going to be a great leader! Your friend, John C. Maxwell."

At that very moment in 1993, I saw my future. I was destined to be a career executive assistant who would one day write a leadership book for assistants. Actually, that's not even close to the future I saw—I thought I was going to be a baseball player. But that note from my buddy John left an imprint on me. I remember thinking, "Me, a leader? Wow. I thought only the rich, famous, or powerful were leaders."

If you've had similar doubts about your leadership potential, it's time for a paradigm shift. Assistant, you are a leader. No matter how far along you are in your career, you're about to tap into a practical resource that will empower and equip you to lead well without burning out.

But before you dive in, here are a few guidelines for getting the most out of this book.

TAKE ADVANTAGE OF BONUS MATERIAL

I reference many resources throughout the book and want you to find them easily. Instead of listing a bunch of unique URLs that are a pain to manually type into your browser or that could become broken links at some point, I've created a go-to website with links to bonus material, articles, and other resources mentioned in the book.

Visit **leaderassistantbook.com/bonus** to dig deeper as you read along.

CONNECT AND SHARE

As you engage with the book, I'd love to hear from you! Ask questions, share feedback, or just say hi at **leaderassistant. com/contact** or email me at **hello@leaderassistant.com**. Also, let me know your favorite quotes from the book by sharing them on social media using the hashtags **#LeaderAssistant** and **#AssistantsLEAD**.

TAKE A SECOND LOOK

If you find yourself thinking, "This won't work in my context," as you read certain sections, don't default to skipping them.

Instead, take a second look. Ask yourself, "What about this section *will* work in my context?" Leader Assistants always look for ways to learn and apply things to their work—even if there are no obvious applications at first glance.

JUMP AROUND AS NEEDED

If, however, you've turned to this book because you're struggling with something in particular, feel free to jump straight to that topic's chapter to get immediate help. For example, if you're burned out, flip over to chapter 23. If you're overwhelmed with managing your executive's calendar, start at chapter 10.

I hope you read the entire book. But it's meant to help you in your role today, so jump around as needed.

DON'T LET TERMS TRIP YOU UP

You might refer to your executive as your "manager," or "leader," or "boss," or "CEO," or something entirely different. Additionally, you might support more than one executive. To keep things consistent and simple throughout the book, I'll refer to the person(s) you support in your role as a singular "executive."

In other words, don't let the title or terms I use trip you up. The tactics in this book apply to assistants who support several executives just as much as they apply to assistants who support one.

THIS BOOK IS NOT ABOUT YOUR TITLE

Numerous variables influence your title: your company's structure, size, industry, location, as well as your years of experience, to name a few. Because of this, I chose to be title-agnostic throughout the book and simply use "Assistant." If your title is Executive Business Partner, Chief of Staff (CoS), Executive Assistant (EA), Office Assistant, Administrative Assistant (AA), Personal Assistant (PA), Senior Administrative Business Partner, Virtual Assistant (VA), Director of Administration, Remote Executive Assistant, or something similar—I wrote this book for you.

THIS BOOK IS FOR EXECUTIVES TOO

Get a copy of this book for your executive and encourage them to read it. Better yet, meet with your executive to discuss the chapters that stand out to you. Talk about the tactics and ideas that will directly impact you both for the better.

If you're an executive reading this, don't highlight parts of the book just so you can ask your assistant, "Why aren't you like this?" Instead, buy the book for your assistant, ask them to read it, then meet together to review insights and share ideas on how you can apply these lessons to your partnership.

THIS BOOK IS YOUR TRAIL GUIDE

This book will help you (re)discover your passion for the assistant profession as you own your role as a Leader Assistant. I've organized it into four parts: the *Four Pillars of a Confident, Game-Changing Assistant.*

PILLAR 1: EMBODY THE CHARACTERISTICS

Pillar 1 is all about *embodying the characteristics* of a Leader Assistant. I'll touch briefly on essential qualities every assistant should have, but the main focus will be the game-changing characteristics you can incorporate to take your role to the next level.

PILLAR 2: EMPLOY THE TACTICS

Identifying the traits of a confident assistant is a good start, but a Leader Assistant also knows how to *employ the right tactics*. In Pillar 2, I'll walk through the tactics that will help you execute your duties better and reach your career goals.

PILLAR 3: ENGAGE IN RELATIONSHIPS

Pillar 3 contains insights and encouragement to help you *engage in relationships*. I'll shed light on traumatic relational experiences common to assistants, myself included. I'll then provide suggestions for navigating the variety of relationships you encounter at work.

PILLAR 4: EXERCISE SELF-CARE

The first three pillars won't get you far if you don't *exercise self-care*. An assistant's job is to support others, and that mentality is probably core to who you are. But supporting others can become your identity to the detriment of your mental, physical, spiritual, and emotional health. In Pillar 4, we'll look at how to support others without sacrificing yourself.

These four pillars are critical if you want to be a game changer. If you neglect them, you'll likely face burnout, stagnation, and anonymity, and your quest to be a leader will come up short.

You are meant for so much more.

THANK YOU

I don't know if I'm supposed to tell you this, but I'm going to because that's how I roll. You're reading an unfinished book. In fact, not only is this book unfinished, I am. The doubts I've faced, and continue to face, throughout this project are overwhelming. My emotional health has been tested as I take the vulnerable step of sharing ideas and lessons learned from my years as an executive assistant, trainer, and coach.

It's nerve-wracking to think about finalizing the manuscript. I fear a ton of ground-breaking and inspirational ideas will flow out of me as soon as the book is published. Not to mention, what I say in this book is out in the world for good—for better or for worse. But if I were to refrain from sharing until I'd perfected the role, I'd never share my ideas. In a similar way, if you wait until you feel like a leader before you begin leading, you'll never start.

But the fact that you're reading this right now means you're ready to join me on this vulnerable journey toward embracing our role as leaders.

So thank you for taking a risk by trusting me with your valuable time. May this book encourage and challenge us both as we seek to be the confident, game-changing Leader Assistants the world needs.

PROLOGUE

ANDREWS GLACIER

—

Location: Andrews Glacier in Rocky Mountain National Park near Estes Park, CO

Elevation: 11,000+ feet above sea level

My sixteen-year-old self watched my fourteen-year-old brother lose his grip, slide down the Colorado mountain glacier, kick his heels into the ice in a desperate attempt to stop, then vanish into a crevasse.

Our group had just hiked four hours up Flattop Mountain to Hallett Peak, and our return route included crossing Andrews Glacier before beginning our descent. My dad, brothers, and I were with a couple we'd just met who offered to be our guides for the day. They weren't professional mountain-trail guides, but they were Colorado residents and owned a Toyota 4Runner.

My brothers and I were dressed for the late August weather: shorts, T-shirts, treadless tennis shoes, and light jackets. Hiking in the summer is great because you can pack light, and it's nice and warm until you get above the tree line. It's windy and freezing at the top, but since we don't typically stay up there for long, we tough it out.

In the dead of winter, Andrews Glacier is frozen solid and packed tight with snow. We'd seen dozens of pictures of people taking leisurely strolls across the snow-covered glacier. However, we soon discovered that in the summer, Andrews Glacier is an entirely different beast. During the day, the sun melts the top layer. Overnight, the bitter cold causes the top layer to freeze again. Instead of a "hard pack" trail that day, the surface was nothing more than a sheet of ice with streams of water trickling down.

Ignoring the "Hidden or open crevasses. Descend with extreme caution." signs, we stepped onto Andrews Glacier. At first, it wasn't too steep, so we had good traction. Several minutes later, the incline sharpened and our treadless shoes could barely grip the ice. We considered turning back, but realized we were already halfway across the glacier. To get more traction, we sat down and scooted on our rear ends.

After a few long minutes, we stopped to reorient ourselves. We were cold, wet, and scared. We were stuck in the middle of a giant glacier, with no confidence in our ability to travel the next few feet, let alone make it across. My dad did what many do when their life is in danger: He said a quick prayer asking God to guide and protect us the rest of the way.

A few seconds after my dad said, "Amen," Jacob slipped and disappeared into the ice. "Jacob!" I screamed. "JACOB!" There was no response for what seemed like hours. Time froze and my heart sank. Would I ever see my brother again? Would I be able to stop *my* fall if I slipped?

The silence broke with a faint but clear "Get me outta here!" We could barely hear Jacob's cries because he had slid so far from us. Our de facto guide slowly worked his way down to my brother, then reached out his hand to help Jacob out of the gap in the ice. (Jacob later told us that when he fell into the crevasse, he landed on a ledge of snow. When he took a step to climb out, the snow collapsed underneath his foot and all he could see was black.)

As Jacob emerged, we were thankful and relieved he was alive. However, our relief quickly turned to doubt as reality hit us square in our cold faces. We still had at least another hour of carefully inching our way across the ice, hoping our footing would hold.

We were in the middle of a dangerous glacier with no proper equipment, no professional trail guide, and no idea whether our next step would hold or be the end of us. We were colder and damper than before, and I was shaken to my core. I'll never forget the fear and uncertainty I felt in that moment as I doubted my ability to survive. The confidence that got me up the mountain was gone.

A CAREER GLACIER

Location: My home office in St. Louis, MO

Elevation: About 500 feet above sea level

Fast-forward sixteen years. My executive is suddenly fired. I'd been his assistant for six years and worked at the organization he founded for twelve. I went from thinking I'd be there for twelve more years to suddenly wondering where I'd be in twelve days. Should I leave the organization to which I'd given everything? Or should I stay to see how the reorg shakes out?

With my executive gone, I had time for some long-overdue self-reflection. And I realized that work had been my life. I was burned out. I needed to reset.

After many sleepless nights, I decided it was time to move on. I knew leaving would not be easy, but I had a vision to guide me: I wanted to be healthy, and I wanted to help other assistants and executives do the same. So I resigned and set out to turn this newfound vision into a business.

Several days later, while looking out my garage office window at my wife, Meg, and our toddlers, Weston and Silas, playing in the yard, I felt panic rising in my chest. Most businesses fail. Even the ones that succeed generally take a few years or more to turn a profit. How would I support my family in the meantime? We decided to sell our house and downsize our life to lower our expenses. But I still needed a full-time day job while I built my business on the side.

I had no resume, no network, and no alternative stream of income to buffer our finances. I lacked experience in the for-profit world and had no community of assistants to lean on. I went from thinking I was ready for an adventure to lacking the confidence to take the next step. I was shaken to the core *again*. I thought I was prepared, but when reality hit, I froze—just like I'd done on Andrews Glacier sixteen years before.

After regrouping, I decided to put one calculated step in front of the other. I put together a resume. I started to network. I launched a blog. And as I did, the missteps that led to my burnout and subsequent feeling of freefall became evident. I'd neglected relationships, thinking I didn't need people. I'd thought taking care of my executive was more important than taking care of myself. I'd failed to learn more tactics to develop myself. And I had an incomplete understanding of what makes an assistant a game-changing leader.

I wrote this book to help you avoid making the same mistakes I did.

You'll face many glaciers of all shapes and sizes throughout your career. Some you'll see a mile away, but others will surprise you. A glacier can be a job change, like it was for me, or it can be a deadline that gets moved up, a promotion, an executive who micromanages, a toxic coworker, a high-pressure project, a complicated calendar, a recession, or an intense negotiation with a vendor.

Being a Leader Assistant is not for the faint of heart. If you're looking for a "cruise control" option, look elsewhere. However, if you want the confidence and ability to conquer glaciers— while other assistants avoid them—you're in the right place.

PILLAR 1

EMBODY THE CHARACTERISTICS

Leader Assistants embody essential and game-changing characteristics.

I thought I was a game changer in my first assistant role because people told me how great I was at my job. They'd regularly thank me for my tireless behind-the-scenes work. However, once I left that bubble, my weaknesses became glaringly obvious. I met a few true Leader Assistants and discovered I had so much to learn.

For example, I thought being humble meant saying yes to everything. As a result, I far too often used humility to justify some of the ridiculous tasks I performed for others. That included requests such as cleaning gutters on a steep roof I had no business being on, mopping up a basement flooded by a septic tank, towing an old pontoon boat with a Jet Ski…and other things I'd prefer to leave out of print.

In other words, my idea of what a Leader Assistant looked like was incomplete. Mastering essentials such as being trustworthy and organized helped me be a good assistant, but it didn't help me be a Leader Assistant. I learned that if I wanted to truly lead, I needed to embody more than just the essentials. I needed to embody the game-changing characteristics too.

As you read on, you might be overwhelmed at the expectations placed upon you. That's OK. When this happens, remember the goal isn't overnight perfection. The goal is incremental improvements over the lifespan of your career.

Let's first dive into the essentials, then work our way up to the game-changing characteristics.

ONE

THE ESSENTIAL CHARACTERISTICS

———

A Leader Assistant has courage, persistence, and a good sense of humor. They stay on top of their game by staying on top of their education. They sharpen their axe by mentoring others. They're a mind reader, diplomat, psychologist, politician, strategic partner, and team player.

—LAUREE C., EXECUTIVE ASSISTANT (SAN DIEGO, CA)

Lists of essential characteristics to embody, whether you're a new assistant or a veteran, are commonplace. Because everyone has their own ideas, I wanted to outline what I see as the essentials for assistants. Think of this as a warmup and a refresher.

As you work your way through the rest of the book, you'll notice many of these traits woven throughout.

PROACTIVE

Being proactive is similar to being able to anticipate, but the difference is important to understand. Being proactive means you plan ahead and prepare for something you *know* is going to happen. However, when you make an educated guess that something *could* happen, and you prepare for it, you're anticipating.

Here's an example of being proactive. Your executive is speaking at a conference, and their presentation has some unusual requirements. You seek out the audio/video (A/V) team for the event weeks in advance so you can explain your executive's needs, and so the A/V team has more time to prepare.

You're expected to be multiple steps ahead of your executive, so don't wait for them to tell you what to do. Be proactive.

RESPONSIVE

Of course, it's impossible to plan for everything, so be ready to quickly tackle problems as they arise. In scenarios where something comes up that was neither planned for nor anticipated, be willing to set aside your proactive hat and put on your responsive one.

In my first year at Capacity (the artificial intelligence software company I work for), I applied for my executive to compete in a startup competition for Ashton Kutcher's venture capital firm, Sound Ventures. After a couple of interviews with them, we didn't hear anything for a few weeks, so we assumed we didn't make the cut.

But five days before the event, we found out that we made the top five and that my executive was scheduled to pitch our company to Kutcher, Matthew McConaughey, Marc Benioff (CEO of Salesforce), Gary Vaynerchuk (CEO of VaynerMedia), and Melody McCloskey (CEO of StyleSeat) at South by Southwest

(SXSW) in Austin, Texas. It was an amazing opportunity for a young startup, but we had only a few days to get ready.

I scrambled to cancel or move almost every meeting that week so my executive could prepare his pitch. I booked flights, hotel rooms, and rental cars for four of our team members to go with my executive. Did I mention SXSW is the busiest event of the year in Austin? Most transportation and lodging options weren't available anymore. Talk about needing to quickly respond in the moment.

We didn't win the competition, but our team got to go to the Snoop Dogg after-party. The next time you see me at an event, remind me to tell you a funny story about that.

LOYAL

As a Leader Assistant, you're committed to the organization and loyal to your executive. You prioritize tasks that come from your executive over tasks that come from someone else. Your executive is your number one priority at work, and they should not question your commitment to them. For example, if I'm meeting with another team member when my executive calls me, I always excuse myself to answer the phone.

If you have an executive who hasn't set clear expectations in this area, I recommend clarifying your job description with them as soon as possible. For example, if you're equally split between two or three executives, the dynamic will be different than if you're an assistant to one executive while supporting other executives as needed.

TRUSTWORTHY

An executive must be able to trust you and your ability to manage confidential information. You hold the keys to their kingdom, so don't lose them. No executive wants an assistant to gossip about them at a dinner party. No board wants an assistant to share private revenue numbers with assistants at other companies. Earn the trust of your executive by maintaining confidentiality at all times.

OTHERS-CENTERED

The assistant role is not a glamorous one. If you've been an assistant for even a few weeks, you're well aware of this. Your job requires hours and hours of behind-the-scenes work, most of which no one—not even your executive—will see.

If you want to be the center of attention, being an assistant isn't the career for you.

Your job is to further the goals and agenda of your executive and company—not your own. (We'll talk about how your goals should align with theirs later.) In the workplace, pay more attention to your executive and other team members than you do to yourself.

I'm not saying you shouldn't take care of yourself. In fact, paying attention to self-care is critical if you want to have the energy and ability to help others. There's a reason Pillar 4 is dedicated to self-care.

I *am* saying try not to take it personally if your executive closes a seven-figure sales contract you played a big role in and fails to thank you when they make the big announcement in front of the entire company. Being a leader means you celebrate the success of others more than your own. Whether you need to make copies for a meeting or lead an important sales demo on behalf of your executive, be happy to help and excited to contribute. A "woe is me" attitude will not cut it.

However, be careful not to let your executive abuse their authority. An effective executive will delegate challenging and interesting projects and tasks, as well as necessary, mundane chores. They'll pay attention to the details so they don't have to bother you on a Sunday morning just to ask for information you sent them on Friday. They'll leave you alone on your days off. An executive worth keeping will be grateful that you put aside your desires to help them and the team.

SOCIABLE

This characteristic is a given for all team members, but especially assistants. Your executive and teams spend a lot of time with you. You're often the first contact for VIP guests, board members, investors, and potential clients. It's important to be personable, kind, and have a good sense of humor.

However, being social and friendly doesn't mean you must be an extrovert to be a Leader Assistant. In fact, introverts make some of the best assistants. We like to sit by ourselves in a quiet office and get stuff done. Meanwhile, our extroverted team members enjoy small talk and socializing with coworkers—even if it distracts them from getting work done. Can you tell I'm letting my introverted bias seep into this section?

I'm a high introvert with developed extroverted skills, and my current and previous executives have been high extroverts. This works well for a strong, complementary partnership. If you're an introvert, you might work better with an extroverted executive who knows how to respect your need for space, and vice versa. But no matter your personality type, being kind to and sociable with others is a must.

ORGANIZED

Many people hire an assistant because they need help getting organized, but others are highly structured and simply spend too much time on the wrong tasks.

For example, executives have better things to do than adding details to their calendar or entering data into a spreadsheet. Their time is better spent meeting with key staff, reading books that inspire them, working on strategic plans, and creating powerful and engaging content for the next board presentation, sales meeting, or investor update.

Synthesize everything your executive throws at you into prioritized tasks and projects, and execute those projects with little oversight. You won't make it long if you were hired because you "have a great personality" or "work really hard" but you can't keep your own car clean.

FLEXIBLE

I've seen assistants with many of the characteristics listed in this chapter, but they lack flexibility. Instead of being excited about and embracing change, they freeze and panic. Early on in my career, this was me. I hated last-minute changes and would get dejected because all the work I put into a project seemed to be all for naught. However, I now realize pivoting can be a good thing, and the process of flexing on the fly can teach us more than staying the course. Instead of seeing work thrown out the window at the last moment as pointless, I started to view "wasted" work as part of the process, helping me improve at my job.

Odds are your executive loves to change things up at the last minute. I think it's a job requirement for all supervisors to frequently scrap a plan and start over, or tinker with the plan right before a deadline. Rather than panicking when this happens, assistants must be ready to adapt.

ASSERTIVE

You can't be flexible all the time, however. There are times when pushing back is an appropriate way to help your executive keep a level head. If your executive always changes things at the last minute, they might have an unhealthy pattern that needs to be addressed before everyone burns out and loses trust in them.

Leader Assistants are aware of the right time to be assertive. For example, if you know a last-minute change could mean running a team into the ground, or even losing some of your best team members, speak up! Tell your executive, "We can't change the plan this late in the game," or "It's not worth our time and energy to shift directions. We just need to move forward." These responses aren't easy, but they show you're thinking strategically for the organization, and that your response isn't just a personal preference.

FOCUSED

In today's fast-paced society, where screens are everywhere and notifications are never-ending, staying focused on one thing at a time is more difficult than ever. Most of the high-level executives I've worked with struggle to stay engaged with a single task for a long period of time, so one of the most crucial characteristics an assistant must possess is the ability to focus. A Leader Assistant can simultaneously focus on their tasks while helping their executive stay on point.

Pay extra-close attention to chapter 9 if you struggle to focus.

DETAIL-ORIENTED

As an assistant, it's your job to notice the details. You can't wait for others to notice.

If your executive is about to present to the board of directors and they have a huge piece of spinach in between their two front teeth, tell them. If a coworker posts a picture on Instagram that inadvertently included a confidential revenue chart on the wall behind them, take care of it. Be aware if your executive's flight was moved to a different departure gate, or if their passport expires a week before their international trip. Don't overlook the details.

NEVER ASSUMES ANYTHING

As I recall the many times I missed a detail because I assumed someone else was on it, I'm reminded of a former coworker's advice: "Never assume anything, Jeremy."

In other words, anytime you find yourself thinking, "I'm sure someone else took care of that," or "I'm positive she understood what I was asking," or in the case of the million-dollar typo

I'll tell you about later, "I'm sure the other two team members would've caught something major if there was anything wrong," double-check your work and pay extra-close attention to the details. When we assume, we miss details.

POSITIVE ATTITUDE

This is pretty straightforward, but a Leader Assistant is someone who has a positive attitude. It isn't always easy, but staying positive no matter what is thrown your way is a characteristic any executive would want in their assistant.

STRONG COMMUNICATION SKILLS

Assistants communicate with coworkers, board members, executives, other assistants, vendors, clients, potential clients, and more. Having strong verbal, nonverbal, and written communication skills is a necessity if you want to thrive as an assistant. We'll discuss tactics for communication in chapter 18.

CURIOUS

You don't have to be an expert in every single topic under the sun, but effective assistants are curious. When you hear a term you don't know, look it up. When someone shows you how to do something, ask them why it's done that way. Be eager to learn and explore. Curiosity not only helps you execute tasks as they come, but also helps you expand your overall knowledge.

RESOURCEFUL

One way to be a resourceful assistant is to figure things out on your own. But if you find yourself stuck on a problem, don't be afraid to ask for help. Leaders aren't afraid to admit they're struggling to solve a problem.

Sometimes outsourcing is the quickest and best way to overcome a glacier. When a project requires expertise in a certain skill set, hire a specialist. For example, I've outsourced projects to human resources experts, lawyers, event planners, graphic designers, even carpenters.

EFFICIENT

I'm always noticing how inefficient things are. I'll be in line at a fast food restaurant, and I'll tell my boys how I'd change things. I'll walk them through which systems are slowing things down, and how I would make them better.

Look for ways to cut seconds out of your work processes. Always ask yourself the question, "How can I minimize wasted time and maximize productivity?" Leader Assistants work quickly and efficiently.

CONTEXT-AWARE

The last essential characteristic is the ability to understand the environment you're in, and adjust accordingly. In other words, Leader Assistants are context-aware.

When you learned how to drive a car, you thought the hard part was simply controlling the vehicle. As you mastered the art of avoiding curbs, however, you learned the real challenge of driving is making decisions based on the many variables surrounding you. Is the road slick from rain or ice? Does the semi-truck see you passing? Is that pedestrian going to step out in front of you? Decisions shouldn't be made in a vacuum.

DO YOU EMBODY THE ESSENTIALS?

One of my former executives went through several assistants before he hired me. The longest any of them lasted was eighteen months. One assistant was loyal but not organized; he was willing to drop anything for his executive, but he also frequently dropped the ball. Another was organized but wasn't proactive; he could keep track of all his tasks, but he would sit around waiting for things to do. It's no wonder they didn't last long.

Making a positive and powerful impact as an assistant requires embodying more than just a few of the essential characteristics. Take a look at the list again, make an honest self-evaluation about which are strengths and which are weaknesses, and pick a few "trouble spots" to work on in the coming weeks.

- Proactive
- Responsive
- Loyal
- Trustworthy
- Others-Centered
- Sociable
- Organized
- Flexible
- Assertive
- Focused
- Detail-Oriented
- Never Assumes Anything
- Positive Attitude
- Strong Communication Skills

- Curious
- Resourceful
- Efficient
- Context-Aware

Use questions like "What would it mean for me to be curious this week?" or "How can I embody assertiveness today?" to get you thinking.

OK. Now that you're caught up on the essentials of your assistant role, let's look at the characteristics that will help you change the game.

TWO

THE GAME-CHANGING CHARACTERISTICS

———

A Leader Assistant has integrity, drive, resilience, compassion, focus, never-ending learning, vision, and the flexibility to start/ stop/start/stop a project (patience at its best).

—SHARI K., EXECUTIVE ASSISTANT (OMAHA, NE)

Being a die-hard Kansas City Royals baseball fan has taught me a lot about what it means to be a game-changing assistant.

The Royals won the World Series in 1985, but I was only one year old, so I don't remember it. Unfortunately, I do remember the decades of losing that followed; it took twenty-nine years for them to return to the playoffs.

The Royals had a handful of good teams in between, including the 1994 squad. In August of that year, ten-year-old me sat in the car on the way to baseball practice as giddy as ever. I was looking forward to talking to my fellow teammates about how good the Royals were doing. They had just won fourteen games in a row and were (in my mind) on their way to making the playoffs. In fact, being the ultimate optimist, I knew they were destined to win the World Series.

As soon as we pulled up to the park, I jumped out of the car, raced up the hill, and started praising the Royals to my teammates. "Guys, the Royals are so good right now! They're the best team in baseball!"

They rolled their eyes at me. "Dude, it doesn't matter how good they are," one of them replied. "Baseball is going to have a strike. The season is almost over, and they aren't even going to have the playoffs. Chill out."

"No way!" I quickly shot back. "They won't cancel the season! They'll work it out and keep playing and the Royals are going to win it all. You watch!"

I can't remember what their responses were exactly, but I got the message: none of my teammates had hope. Yet I remained hopeful that a strike would not be happening. How could they take baseball away from me?

The Royals' win streak ended that day, and in fact, they ended up losing four out of their next five games. But I just knew they would break out for another winning streak soon. Unfortunately, I was wrong. On Thursday, August 11, 1994, the big bad world (aka MLB owners) took baseball away from me. The players went on strike, and they wouldn't end up playing again until the following season. My tall, skinny, three-sizes-too-big Royals T-shirt-wearing, Wiffle ball-pitching self was heartbroken. My Little League teammates were right, and I was devastated.

I experienced twenty more years of heartbreak after that awful childhood moment. When the Royals finally made the play-offs in 2014 and 2015, I took advantage of the opportunity and attended every home playoff game.

But loyalty and perseverance aren't the only lessons I've gleaned from my fandom.

My favorite player during the Royals' amazing run of back-to-back World Series appearances was their center fielder, Lorenzo Cain. He was fast, athletic, and exciting to watch. He had the essentials down, but there was something extra special about Cain. He could change a game with one play, and did so many times. When Cain was playing, I didn't look away, afraid I'd miss an impossible diving catch or a home-run-robbing grab against the wall.

In one of those thrilling playoff games, Cain made a couple of diving catches back-to-back. Meg, my brother Kyle, my dad Bill, and I were sitting in the front row, up against the fence in left-center field. We had an up-close-and-personal view of Cain's amazing plays from our great seats.

Meg pointing to Lorenzo Cain from our seats.

"Game changing" is the best descriptor of Cain during those two years. In fact, 2015 was Cain's best year by Wins Above Replacement (WAR): a stat that measures a player's total contribution to his team.

What made Cain a game changer? Was it his speed? There are plenty of fast athletes who aren't elite. How about his work ethic? That sure helped, but even many subpar athletes work hard.

Here are some game-changing characteristics Cain embodied:

- His ability to discern where the ball would end up as a hitter made contact so he could take the appropriate first step.
- His steadiness in high-pressure situations.
- His confidence that he had what it took to make the catch.

ARE YOU A GAME CHANGER?

Do you exhibit the game-changing characteristics Cain had? The best baseball players in the world embody some of the same characteristics as the best assistants in the world. Executives don't just want a solid team member—they want a risk-taking game changer.

These are the five game-changing characteristics of a Leader Assistant:

- Discerning
- Steady
- Confident
- Humble
- Future-Proof

In the following chapters, we'll delve into what each of these characteristics is, and how to embody them.

THREE

DISCERNING

—

Leader Assistants possess the confidence to make considerate and informed decisions that lead to fruitful actions—in the absence of executive presence.

—KRISTI D., EXECUTIVE ASSISTANT (SAN JOSE, CA)

Game-changing Leader Assistants are discerning. As Oxford defines it, *discerning* means "having or showing good judgment." There are many ways this characteristic can play out in your role, but I'm going to focus on two: anticipating the needs of your executive, and making decisions on their behalf.

ANTICIPATE THE NEEDS OF YOUR EXECUTIVE

"What's one thing you wish your assistant could do?" I've asked dozens of executives this question. And every single one of them said they wish their assistant could read their mind. In other words, they want an assistant who anticipates what's needed, long before it's needed.

Thinking five or six steps ahead is critical for assistants. Why?

Because our executives are always thinking ahead. So plan for what's coming next week, next month, even next year.

Remember what I said before: Being proactive means planning for something that's scheduled to happen. Anticipating means planning for something that might never happen. For example, booking a flight for a planned trip six months from now is proactive. That's essential, but it's not game changing.

Anticipating your executive's needs means you book a backup flight for the next morning because **(a)** the weather is typically awful in January, **(b)** your executive has a critical board meeting they can't miss, or **(c)** their primary flight departs toward the end of rush hour, so there's a high likelihood they'll get stuck in traffic and miss the flight.

Anticipation is a game-changing characteristic because it requires you to consider and analyze unlikely scenarios your executive still might need you to handle. If you struggle to anticipate, ask your executive to share their long-term goals and ideas with you. If you know what their "big picture" is, you can better shape their "little picture" to match.

The best mind readers are in the same room as the mind they're trying to read. Sit down with your executive on a regular basis to go over their top three goals for the next week, month, and quarter. Discuss what needs to happen to accomplish these goals, and write out action items for each.

Another way to better anticipate your executive's needs is to spend time every week looking ahead a few weeks, months, even a year, then working your way back. Your executive doesn't have time to look at every detail of a trip four months from now. That's why they have you.

If you've tried to anticipate in the above ways but still seem to be a few steps behind, consider seeking help from outside training and coaching. If that still doesn't help, you might need a new executive. Or, perhaps the administrative profession is not the right fit for you.

MAKE GOOD DECISIONS

Your executive makes decisions all day, every day, so any time you can make a decision for them, do it. Be decisive to protect your executive from getting a serious case of decision fatigue.

Game-changing assistants are always ready to make decisions. You can start by making several small choices throughout the day, like what to get them for lunch, which conference room to book for their upcoming brainstorming meeting, or whether to reply to that random LinkedIn message.

Once you've proven capable of handling small decisions, your executive will trust your judgment on more critical matters. I've influenced key decisions during my career as an assistant, affecting things such as product updates, a company rebrand, and hiring and firing. Twice, my company faced a tough decision on which office to move the team to. In both instances, my executive looked at me and asked, "Which office do you think we should choose?" I quickly gave my answer, as well as my justifications for it. Each time, he said, "OK, let's do it."

Unfortunately, I didn't always speak up when I had a gut feeling. I didn't feel good about several employee hires that, down the road, turned into awful situations I could've helped us avoid. We interviewed a candidate for a major leadership role at my previous organization. He gave off a bad vibe when we interacted. I thought he was inauthentic and putting on a show to land the job. However, I didn't say anything—partly because I knew how important it was for us to fill the role, but also because I didn't trust my gut.

We ended up hiring the guy and it went OK for a few months. But it quickly went downhill when it turned out he wasn't the kind of person he made himself out to be. He was supposed to be leading a team, but everyone eventually saw right through his façade. He was lazy and failed to keep his promises. We fired him, but it took years for that team to recover.

If you have a bad feeling about something or someone, don't dismiss it. Your insight is valuable.

How can you improve your decision-making skills? Start by making suggestions to your executive. It could be as simple as recommending a template for the board slides. Get your executive's feedback to determine whether your views on the template align. Rinse and repeat with other suggestions until your decisions match theirs more often than not.

Your job is to free up your executive so they have more bandwidth to focus on decisions only they can make. With practice, the number of decisions only they can handle will decrease, and your value to the company will increase.

GAME-CHANGING QUESTIONS
FOR SELF-REFLECTION

Reflect on your ability to anticipate and make good decisions by considering these questions:

- What are some upcoming situations I could think through for my executive? What unlikely scenarios do I need to plan for?

- In what areas do I struggle to read my executive's mind? What steps can I make this week to better anticipate their needs?

- When was the last time I made the wrong decision? What did I miss in that situation?

- What's a decision I can make for my executive this week?

- Have I ever allowed something negative to happen to my company because I stayed quiet about my concerns? Why did I doubt myself?

FOUR

STEADY

—

Have you ever seen a professional juggler juggling knives? They never drop them, and they never stop smiling. Assistants are similar to knife jugglers. They have the ability to juggle multiple projects and never let others see the stress they may be under. Assistants are leaders not because of their ability to do a lot at once, but because of their posture while doing those tasks.

—DAVID B., EXECUTIVE ASSISTANT AND INTERIM HR DIRECTOR (INDIAN WELLS, CA)

One of my coworkers repeatedly asks me how I'm so calm during stressful times at work. For the longest time, I had no idea how to respond. I've always been a fairly steady person. Meg even calls me "Steady Slim" (I have a tall and skinny physique, in case you didn't know). But my coworker's question got me thinking: "How do I remain so steady in the storms around me?"

After some reflection, I unlocked three keys to my steadiness: I enjoy the process, I entertain the worst-case scenario, and I embrace the tension.

Before we dive into these attributes, however, I want to make a quick distinction.

I was going to call this game-changing characteristic "calm in the chaos," but I like the word *steady* better. Why? Because sometimes you have to get a little upset in the midst of the madness to get something done. Sometimes you need to raise your intensity to move the needle.

If you're a parent, you know what it's like for a kid to not pay attention unless you use a certain tone. If your three-year-old steps onto a busy street with oncoming traffic, you can't afford to remain calm. You have to be fierce and push everything aside as you race to snag your child out of harm's way. But your lack of calm in those moments doesn't mean you're unsteady. In fact, your steady intensity is what allows you to perform your super-parent mission.

The following three keys help me remain steady in the stressful storms of the workplace.

ENJOY THE PROCESS

I happen to like the crazy. It keeps me interested and engaged. I enjoy solving problems when it's hard to think straight. I enjoy the occasional late-night work session to get a new feature out for a client. The highs and lows of startup life are tough to handle, but one thing is true: there's never a dull moment—especially as an executive assistant.

If you don't learn to enjoy the process, you'll struggle to remain steady. You'll always be dreaming of the future, which will leave you stressed out by a present that doesn't match it. If enjoying the process doesn't come naturally to you, stay connected to the big picture. Setting your sights on your company's mission can help you roll with the complex process required to achieve it.

You can also think critically about common processes and identify ways to make them more efficient. You'll always face unexpected changes, but if you can streamline things as much as possible, the process won't be nearly as stressful.

ENTERTAIN THE WORST-CASE SCENARIO

This might seem a bit morbid, but another tactic that helps me remain steady is to remind myself that I'm not dead.

No matter how stressful things are at work, things could be worse. If I lose my job, life will be difficult, but I can find new work. Life is too short to make my career the most important part of my life, or to let a stressful situation cause me to freak out. Instead, I do my best to entertain the worst-case scenario.

If I'm not dead, then I have every reason to be grateful.

I'm not perfect, of course, and neither are you. We all freak out at times. But when we do, it's because we see our circumstances through the lens of ungratefulness. We think to ourselves, "This is the worst," when in reality, it's not. Entertaining the worst-case scenario helps us step back and look at life from a healthier perspective.

EMBRACE THE TENSION

The assistant role is fluid. It's unclear. It's ever-changing. It's not clean-cut and orderly. It's full of tension. You'll constantly be pulled in different directions by executives or team members. Heck, I've received two completely opposite requests from the same executive within a five-minute window. This is the tension all assistants face. Don't run from it. Don't let it shake you. Instead, feed off of the tension. Lean into it.

Being hire number one at a software-as-a-service (SaaS) startup with a CEO who sold his last company for almost a billion dollars presents a lot of opportunities for me to embrace (or run from) tension. My executive approached me with one such opportunity about a month after launching the company. He asked me to oversee accounting, human resources, and operations for the company—not forever, but until we could hire an accountant, director of HR, etc.

I'm an introvert who hates math, yet my new role was going to include working with numbers and people. What could go wrong, right? Of course, I was also expected to fulfill my duties as the CEO's assistant on top of these new responsibilities. In other words, I was going to be working in constant tension.

Instead of running or losing my cool, I replied to his overwhelming request with a hesitant, but honest, response. I let him know I didn't enjoy accounting and that I was bad at math. I also said I didn't like paperwork and that I wasn't the best people person. But I told him I'd run the company—as long as it wasn't a long-term solution.

Thankfully, we now have a much larger team, so I'm able to focus on being an assistant. But during that season of wearing multiple hats, I discovered the more I leaned into the tension, the more confident and steady I became. The more I embraced the stress and anxiety, the more successful I was.

To embrace tension, be aware of it and be ready to discern *which* characteristic to embody in a given moment. The ability to readily set aside one characteristic for its opposite, depending on the situation, will set you apart from the pack.

For example, there's tension in the constant battle between planning ahead but also being ready to respond on the fly. One minute, you're planning an itinerary for four months out. The next minute, you drop everything to head to your executive's house, grab his new driver's license, and drive it to him at the airport because they won't let him through security with an expired ID. (In case you're wondering, I got my executive his ID with time to spare.)

In these moments, you can't say, "Sorry, boss, I'm working on being proactive and planning ahead right now; I can't help you get through security. I operate better when things are less chaotic and on my calendar ahead of time." Good luck with that response.

What if you catch your longtime executive doing something unethical, immoral, or illegal? There's certainly tension there. Suddenly, you're faced with the choice of being loyal to an executive you've supported for years—and who has supported you—or doing the right thing.

Deep down, you know reporting your executive's behavior is the right thing to do, but you get paid well, have great benefits, and enjoy your schedule. You didn't do anything wrong, so why should you lose your job?

Plenty of assistants push things under the rug for these or other reasons, claiming loyalty as their justification. But a Leader Assistant gives up their loyalty to do the right thing.

Take time to identify specific tension builders that are difficult for you to navigate, then work through them. For example, if being proactive is tough because you like to fly by the seat of your pants, develop your proactive muscles by scheduling an hour each week to look ahead at your executive's calendar.

When the tension makes you uneasy, remind yourself of the parts of your life that feel more certain, more comfortable, more settled. Close your eyes and gain some composure by letting your mind go there for a moment. Think of the sense of accomplishment you'll feel when you successfully navigate a difficult situation to reach your goals.

Stick a quote on your desk to think about when you're stuck. I like this one by former UCLA men's basketball coach John Wooden: "Flexibility is the key to stability." Or this anonymous quote: "Be stubborn about your goals, and flexible about your methods."

Will you let the tension hold you back or cause you to stumble? Or will you be steady when it's time to face your own glacier?

GAME-CHANGING QUESTIONS
FOR SELF-REFLECTION

Reflect on your ability to be steady in the storms by considering these questions:

- When was the last time I lost my cool? What triggered it?

- What helps me be steady when things around me fall apart?

- What parts of the process do I enjoy? What parts do I dislike? How can I remedy those problem areas?

- What's a tension holding me back right now that I could embrace instead?

FIVE

CONFIDENT

—

An assistant becomes a leader by building confidence in him/ herself. Confidence is built by will and determination to be the best (personally and professionally), a willingness to work with and learn from others, and the support of others in and outside of your organization (networking).

—REBECCA S., EXECUTIVE ADMINISTRATIVE
ASSISTANT (GREENVILLE, SC)

As an assistant, you're in contact with the most confident and powerful people in your company, city, industry—for some of you, even the world. How can you expect to lead if you lack confidence in your ability to get the job done?

Game-changing Leader Assistants are confident.

I'm not talking about a Lifetime-movie, music-pumping, "I am awesome! I am strong! I am brave!" confidence. What if you're not strong? What if you aren't feeling brave in a given moment? What if you fail today, tomorrow, and the next day?

I'm also not talking about an arrogant, narcissistic, "I do what I want, and don't care what you think!" confidence, like when I'm driving. (Hey, leaders should own their dirt, right?) Or like that time I was at a grocery store with a girl I was trying to impress and I ate a strawberry off the shelf, claiming, "Hey, free strawberry samples!" (They were not free samples, and I did not impress the girl.)

What I'm talking about is a deep-rooted, humble confidence. An unwavering belief that you have what it takes to figure things out, *and* a forgiving grace for yourself if you don't figure things out.

Your confidence naturally will take a hit when you face an unexpected glacier. If you doubt your ability in those moments, you're not alone. The most confident people in the world have doubts, whether they admit it or not.

I've spent more than half my working life as an EA. I've worked with celebrities, professional athletes, billionaires, and C-suite executives at Fortune 100 companies. You'd think I'd be extremely confident anytime I meet a high-level executive. But there are days I question whether I've got what it takes to ask for extra sauce at Chick-fil-A.

There are times I'm confident in my skills, but I'm not confident in my ability to communicate well. Other days I doubt my talent, but not my worth as a person. Some days I'm confident and assertive at work, but when I get home and have to manage my boys' bedtime routine, I lose all confidence.

So, how do we strengthen our self-assurance?

DEVELOP A DEEP-ROOTED, HUMBLE CONFIDENCE

Experience is one way to start. No matter how old or new you are to the assistant role, find someone with more experience (and more confidence), and ask them to help you grow. It can be as simple as grabbing lunch with a fellow assistant to share tips and tricks, as well as trade horror and success stories.

You could also reach out to one of the many amazing assistant coaches on LinkedIn for professional development to help you gain confidence. Conferences and online courses can help you become more assured in your role as well.

But experience, coaching, and training will only get you so far. The key to unlocking a deep-rooted confidence is to remember this:

You are a valuable human being—no matter how good or bad you perform at work.

Until you latch onto this powerful truth, you will lack confidence. If you don't remind yourself of this fact on a regular basis, your confidence will fade as you let the ups and downs at work affect you on a deep, personal level.

"But Jeremy, I don't feel valuable." I get it. I don't feel valuable all the time either. So what destroys our confidence? The lies we've been told, and the lies we tell ourselves.

DON'T BELIEVE THE LIES

What lies have you been told that you've held on to as truths?

Maybe a teacher in high school said you'd never amount to anything. Maybe a coworker said you were incompetent. Maybe your dad didn't encourage or believe in you. These statements can be tough to shake, but they don't define you.

The lies you tell yourself are another confidence destroyer. Lies like "I don't have what it takes," or "I can't do it as well as Susan can," or "They won't listen to me." These lies wreck your confidence. In fact, they're so powerful, you might not recognize the truth when you hear it. Think about the last time you received a compliment. Did you respond with gratitude, or dismiss it, telling yourself it was undeserved?

Almost every day, my son Silas says I'm "the best daddy ever." I know I'm likely not the best dad ever, so at first I would respond with something like "I doubt it, but I do my best." Then I thought about how he means it. To him, I really am the best daddy ever. But I was unwilling to hear it. Even worse, my response was teaching him to reject compliments or kind words from others. So now I simply say, "Thank you, sweetie."

When someone says something nice about you, own it and say thanks. Don't let the negative lies in your head drown out the positive truth.

Another example of a lie in my life was the seemingly small but powerful thought that I'd never be able to enjoy dining at nice restaurants because I'd always be worried about paying my bills.

This lie I told myself was heavily influenced by my family of origin. I grew up in a family of six, and my parents never made much money. Sure, we had food on the table, clothes on our back, and a roof over our heads. But we rarely went out to eat, we shopped at Aldi and Payless Shoes, and we only went on vacation *if* we had a cheap or free place to stay somewhere within driving distance. The pro was I learned a ton about saving money, keeping a budget, and not buying things I can't afford. The con was it took me a long time to learn that it's OK to splurge every now and then.

Eleanor Roosevelt said it well: "No one can make you feel inferior without your consent." This goes for the lies you tell yourself too.

Counseling has helped me process the many ways my family of origin impacts my confidence to this day. Some people attach a stigma to counseling. "Oh, you must be really messed up if you're seeing a therapist." But that's simply not true. Mature people who want to grow and improve seek help in many forms. I highly recommend seeing a good therapist or counselor if you've never seen one. You can't fight back against the lies in your mind, or the lies from others, without outside help.

A Leader Assistant's confidence is not fueled by pride. It's fueled by humility.

SERVE THE WORK

Dorothy Sayers, an English crime writer and poet, wrote an essay called "Why Work?" I find her ideas in this essay fascinating to think about as they relate to how we can be confident in our role.[1] In "Why Work?" Sayers says a worker must "serve the work." This sounds like a recipe for burnout, but hear her out:

> "The moment you think of serving other people, you begin to have a notion that other people owe you something for your pains; you begin to think that you have a claim on the community. You will begin to bargain for reward, to angle for applause, and to harbor a grievance if you are not appreciated. But if your mind is set upon serving the work, then you know you have nothing to look for; the only reward the work can give you is the satisfaction of beholding

1   I was made aware of this wonderful thought from Sayers in Timothy Keller's book, Every Good Endeavor.

its perfection. The work takes all and gives nothing but itself; and to serve the work is a labor of pure love.... It is the work that serves the community; the business of the worker is to serve the work."

If you're "serving the work," as opposed to "angling for applause" from your executive, you won't feel as defeated or be as negatively influenced when your executive doesn't appreciate your amazing work. Your confidence will have deeper roots. You'll no longer do what you do to be recognized. Instead, you'll simply seek to do great work.

Are you placing your professional confidence in what your executive says, or the quality of your work? When you ask for a compensation increase, will you base your business case on your executive's subjective opinion, or on the objective data showing the quality of your work?

Be confident in your ability to figure things out (and be kind to yourself if you can't), your value as a human being (no matter what happens at work), and the quality of your work (not the amount of accolades you receive).

Let's shift our focus to humility—the deepest and strongest root of your confidence as a game-changing Leader Assistant.

GAME-CHANGING QUESTIONS
FOR SELF-REFLECTION

Reflect on your confidence by considering these questions:

- Where do I lack confidence?

- In what environments do I feel most confident?

- Am I confident in some areas, but not others? Why?

- Do I work to receive recognition, or because I enjoy the work?

SIX

HUMBLE

———

An assistant leads in the trenches, working confidently yet humbly, side by side with their executive and peers, not exerting power or control, but influence and diplomacy.

—JAMES S., EXECUTIVE ASSISTANT (CHICAGO, IL)

I like to think I'm a humble person. Then I remember the times I fail to be humble, or the times I'm humbled by my mistakes. Or how much I like to pretend I'm right—even when I'm wrong. Did I mention how hard it is for me to listen to the feedback I receive from coworkers or podcast listeners?

Maybe I'm not so humble after all.

In fact, to keep my pride in check, let's kick off this chapter on humility with a humbling story of a time I made a mistake.

THE MILLION-DOLLAR TYPO

My executive and his business partner were looking to purchase a large office building. When they found one, I was one of four people responsible for editing the offer letter. We made several changes to it, reviewed it a few times, then sent it to the building owners. Our intent was to offer $2.5 million, but thanks to a single typo, we offered $3.5 million for the building.

There's nothing like the feeling of discovering you missed a million-dollar typo. I wasn't the only one to miss the error, but I still felt awful and completely responsible for missing it. After all, I'm the detail-oriented assistant who's supposed to catch these things.

After we corrected the error, I apologized to the parties involved, including my very upset executive. I had to be honest and admit I did not review the letter thoroughly, because I assumed the other parties involved would. It turned out OK in the end (the owners didn't want to sell the building), but I learned *there's nothing more humbling than having to admit when you've made a mistake.*

The truth is, it doesn't matter how confident or capable you are at doing your job—you will screw up. The question is, will you let your mistakes humble you so you can learn from them? Or will your pride get in the way of you becoming a humble leader?

Don't be afraid to admit when you make mistakes.

HOW DO YOU RECEIVE CRITICISM?

Another way to gauge how humble you are—or aren't—is how you receive criticism from others. Do you get defensive as soon as someone suggests you make a change? When was the last time you applied even a small piece of constructive criticism you received? Humble assistants embrace vulnerability by laying down their defenses in the face of criticism.

Criticism stings. But there are things you can do to ease the pain. The next time someone criticizes you, tell them you appreciate their feedback. Let them know you're going to take some time to consider their thoughts. Then remove yourself from the situation. Take a walk, do something you feel confident in, or sleep on it before you come back to it. Remember: It's OK to be wrong or make mistakes, as long as you learn from it.

In new-teacher training, you learn that kids need to hear criticism sandwiched between positive reinforcement. Your critic might not do this, so do it for yourself. Tell yourself something positive you did, think about the criticism, and follow it with another positive.

When you're ready, engage in a thoughtful conversation with the other person. Of course, sometimes the criticism is unhelpful and not worth your time; a simple "Thanks for your note" is more than sufficient in these situations.

You can also head off the discomfort of negative feedback by asking for it. Our pride can't be bruised when we've already acknowledged our need to learn. Try asking, "What could I have done better?" to encourage constructive feedback, not just complaints.

Being humble means asking for, accepting, and applying feedback from others.

THINK OF YOURSELF LESS

As you can see, criticism goes better when you start from a place of humility. So don't sit around waiting until you make a mistake or receive feedback to be humbled. Leaders actively pursue humility. As C. S. Lewis points out in *Mere Christianity*, the first step toward humility is acknowledging your pride:

> "Do not imagine that if you meet a really humble man he will be what most people call 'humble' nowadays: he will not be a sort of greasy, smarmy person, who is always telling you that, of course, he is nobody. Probably all you will think about him is that he seemed a cheerful, intelligent chap who took a real interest in what you said to him. If you do dislike him it will be because you feel a little envious of anyone who seems to enjoy life so easily. He will not be thinking about humility: he will not be thinking about himself at all.

> "If anyone would like to acquire humility, I can, I think, tell him the first step. The first step is to realise that one is proud. And a biggish step too. At least, nothing whatever can be done before it. If you think you are not conceited, it means you are very conceited indeed."

Here's a more succinct version of the above from Rick Warren's *The Purpose Driven Life*:

> "Humility is not thinking less of yourself, but thinking of yourself less."

Devaluing yourself by seeing yourself as not worthy of recognition is not humility. It's false humility, also known as pride. When you're truly humble, you're driven by the work you do for others, not the recognition you receive from them. When recognition does come, you don't well up with pride—you well up with gratefulness.

Be grateful for any opportunity to help others. A Leader Assistant doesn't think, "How can this help me?" A Leader Assistant thinks, "How can I help?"

GAME-CHANGING QUESTIONS FOR SELF-REFLECTION

Reflect on your humility and pride by considering these questions:

- What am I grateful for?

- Where has my pride caused ungratefulness and slowed me down?

- Where have I been prideful in the workplace?

- How can I work to be more humble instead?

SEVEN

FUTURE-PROOF

———

A Leader Assistant is calm, confident, astute, and uses their emotional intelligence to great effect.

—ALISON K., PERSONAL ASSISTANT
(LONDON, UNITED KINGDOM)

Are you prepared for the artificial intelligence (AI) revolution? Should you be scared your job is going to be replaced by AI someday? Yes, and no. Have a healthy fear (i.e., reverence and respect) of AI and other technology, but don't let it keep you up at night.

More and more tasks are handled by machine learning algorithms and automated software. If you ignore this reality, you might not survive the AI revolution. We're a long way from being fully replaced by robots, but AI is infiltrating a growing number of industries and rapidly changing the way many of us work.

For example, I'm an assistant at Capacity—a SaaS company in St. Louis. Our secure, AI-native platform helps teams do their best work by automating key processes and reducing support ticket load. Our chatbot sits on top of the platform with state-of-the-art natural language processing so you don't have to know the precise way to ask for what you need—you just ask. If a coworker wants to know when my executive (our CEO) is free next, they can ask Capacity. If I'm on vacation and my executive is traveling, he can ask Capacity for his airline rewards information, or he can ask for his plumber's phone number if a pipe bursts at his home.

Did you notice something? The tasks Capacity handles aren't ones that typically bring us joy and excitement. Imagine if you could spend more time solving real problems and creating amazing products instead of answering the same mundane questions over and over.

If you want to be a game-changing assistant, you can't let the fear of being replaced by AI paralyze you. Instead, explore how you can use the AI revolution to make yourself more valuable. Seek out tools that give you more time at work to do what you love and what really drives results.

ARTIFICIAL INTELLIGENCE AND THE FUTURE OF ASSISTANTS

I literally watch the AI revolution unfold at the desk across from me, and it can get overwhelming at times. You probably feel the same way when you read the latest article about artificial intelligence automating jobs. My executive puts it bluntly, "Automate before you're automated."

But there's good news: AI will never replace humans. In fact, the future of work is not AI versus humans; it's AI *plus* humans. It will continue to increase our capabilities and productivity.

However, though AI might not replace you, it could make your specific job obsolete. So be on the lookout for ways to reskill and upskill throughout your career if you want to be a Leader Assistant. (I know a longtime assistant who became a knowledge management expert at her company during a major reorg. It was a perfect example of embracing the need to reskill.)

The following four tactics will help you automate and prepare for the future of work.

1. BE AN EARLY ADOPTER

The first way to future-proof your career is to learn about and use new technology as it becomes available—or even better, before it becomes available to the rest of the world. Be an early adopter. Get your hands on the latest software and tools that could help you with some aspect of your job. How? Sign up for free trials, join beta tests, or apply to be a guinea pig for your friend's new project.

Maybe it's exploring an AI platform like Capacity that can schedule meetings, automate onboarding processes, mine policy documents, and answer FAQs. Maybe it's testing an automation tool that can help you quickly audit your executive's time, so you can be more strategic with their schedule. (In chapter 10, we'll look at tracking your executive's time.) Or maybe it's something as simple as using Google Assistant, Alexa, or Siri to set reminders. Whatever it is, be on the hunt for opportunities to use technology that's shaping the future.

If you aren't sure where to look for opportunities to be an early adopter, start by educating yourself. Take a course on artificial intelligence. Listen to a podcast dedicated to machine learning.

Read books and articles about the future of work. If you'd like some guidance, I put together a guide at **leaderassistantbook. com/bonus** to help you kick off your AI learning adventure.

2. DEVELOP YOUR EMOTIONAL INTELLIGENCE

Keeping your human-only skills sharp is another way to future-proof your career. You might be up to speed on all the latest and greatest software, hip to modern business tactics, and crushing it with your leadership skills. But how emotionally aware are you? Can you control the way you express your emotions? Are you able to process the varying emotions you feel? Can you handle relationships empathetically? What have you done to develop your emotional intelligence?

Here are some game-changing tactics you can employ to cultivate your emotional intelligence.

RESPOND, DON'T REACT, TO CONFLICT

To react is to let your emotions get the best of you. When you react to conflict, you say something you'll regret.

To *respond* is to control your emotions, consider the situation, and think about what you're going to say before you say it. When you respond to conflict, you put yourself in the other person's shoes, and thoughtfully share your opinions or suggest a solution.

My dad and I like to face conflict head-on. Growing up, we would yell at each other, talk things through, work things out, and by the end of our heated conversation, the conflict typically would be resolved. One of my former executives dealt with conflict in this way too. If we had a disagreement, we'd react to it ASAP—sometimes loudly—work through it, and move on.

One day, Meg and I were in the middle of a disagreement with her parents. Instead of responding to that specific conflict in a calm and collected manner, I did what I had grown up doing. I let my emotions get the best of me and lashed out at my father-in-law with my opinion and a few choice words. As you can imagine, my reaction did not invite my in-laws to engage in further discussion. I didn't resolve the conflict—I escalated it.

A blowup like this would've sparked a genuine conversation with my dad or former executive. With my father-in-law, it built a wall between us. In other words, I was *not* emotionally intelligent in that moment. I was quite the opposite.

Game-changing, confident Leader Assistants learn to respond to conflict at work, not react.

BE INTENTIONAL WITH YOUR VOCABULARY

Do you think about what you're going to say before you say it? Do you consider whether your words are constructive or destructive? Is your vocabulary vague and full of complaining, or are you specific and helpful?

For example, there's a difference between saying your coworker Jeff is "a bad team member" and saying, "When Jeff shows up late to most meetings, it communicates to the rest of the team that he doesn't value us or respect our time."

Be intentional and thoughtful with your vocabulary. One way to practice this is to write out what you're going to say before you say it. Then read it out loud to hear how your tone comes across.

PROCESS YOUR EMOTIONS

The ability to process your feelings is critical to developing emotional intelligence. Unfortunately, I'm terrible at this. I have a tendency to bury my emotions instead of questioning why I'm feeling them. If I'm sad, I shrug it off and tell myself to get over it. If I'm angry, I lash out without exploring why I felt the need to lash out.

Meg and our counselor have helped me become more self-aware by encouraging me to question the motives behind what I say and do. Why did I gossip about my coworker at lunch or send that scathing email? Was it because I wanted attention? If so, why did I want attention? Or was I afraid to talk to them directly because I have a fear of conflict?

Processing my own emotions is still a battle for me. But discovering and naming the motives behind my emotions has helped me develop self-awareness.

BE EMPATHETIC

Processing your emotions will help you practice empathy toward others. If a coworker is struggling to produce, put yourself in their shoes. Did they recently experience a difficult personal event? Did they just get a new supervisor? Are they simply having a bad day? Empathize with others.

Robots will never know what it's like to be human. They'll never be able to feel your pain, experience your joy, or know how badly you miss a loved one. They'll never be as intuitive as an emotionally aware human being.

AI won't ask how your elderly father is holding up after his hip replacement. A chatbot won't be sensitive to the fact that you were crying in the break room because your cat died. A robot can't offer you a ride when your car breaks down. (OK, maybe in some places it can, but you get the idea.)

Treat humans like they're people who matter, because they *are* people, and they *do* matter. When companies look to trim their head count during a recession, they'll first look at productivity and business impact. But when they're forced to choose between two equally productive team members, they'll pick the more empathetic employee nine times out of ten.

3. LOOK FOR (THE RIGHT) PROBLEMS AND SUGGEST SOLUTIONS

The next way to prepare for the future of work is to look for problems others have yet to solve. As an assistant, you see the good, the bad, and the ugly in your organization. You can complain about what's wrong and let other people figure things out. Or you can use the unique vantage point you have to identify problems and suggest solutions. If you're a self-motivated problem solver who constantly brings solutions to the table, you won't be replaced by AI someday.

But being future-proof is not just about solving problems. It's about *identifying the right problems*. In fact, it's more valuable to suggest the wrong solution to the right problem than it is to provide an amazing solution to the wrong problem.

"But how can I identify the right problems, Jeremy?" I'm glad you asked.

Start with what keeps your executive up at night. What are they concerned about? Look for ways you can alleviate those concerns. Shift your focus toward the issues on their mind. In chapter 21, I share several questions to ask your executive that will help you pinpoint problems worth solving.

Time spent addressing the wrong problem is a waste of time. But repeatedly failing to conquer the right problem is sometimes the only path to progress. Thomas Edison famously said, "I have not failed. I've just found ten thousand ways that won't work." You might as well find the solutions that won't work to help your executive more quickly discover the right solution for the right problem.

4. BE A REVENUE GENERATOR

If you want to be future-proof, be one of the best salespeople in your company. Always be on the lookout for ways to impact the bottom line. If your company fails to increase revenue or raise enough money, you and your coworkers will be out of work, so don't sit around waiting for tasks to hit your inbox.

If you've never seen yourself as a revenue generator, it's time to change your perspective. (This still applies to you if you work at a nonprofit, by the way, so don't skip ahead.) Future-proof assistants lead by example and get those around them excited to help their company grow. If you're not excited to help your organization grow, and don't believe in what they're doing, figure out why quick.

There are a few ways to step up your sales game.

First, know your company's mission, vision, and sales pitch like the back of your hand. If you don't know it, invite yourself to sales meetings so you can soak up the info. Learn how to give the pitch yourself by reading all the onboarding guides for account executives. Read the fundraising prospectus your executive just asked you to send to potential donors. The goal is to confidently and succinctly describe your organization's mission and/or product to a stranger on an elevator, or to that business-owner friend who could be a future customer.

Speaking of friends who run a business, I sourced and helped close our young startup's first multiyear contract—with a company run by a friend of mine. I'm not sharing this to gloat. I'm sharing this as a challenge to you. Who do you know that could benefit from your company's product or service? Take them to lunch and see what happens. If you believe in what your organization is doing, why not share it with your network?

Second, grow your influence to increase your company's brand awareness. One of Capacity's sales team members sent me an email from an assistant in my network. This assistant was going to delete a sales email she received from Capacity, but because she follows me on LinkedIn and appreciates what I do for the assistant community, she forwarded the email to her executive. My influence directly helped our sales team. In chapter 20, we'll look at ways you can grow your influence and, in turn, build trust and credibility for your organization's brand.

Another way to step up your sales game is to study the psychology of sales. Learn to listen to and understand a potential customer's pain points. Be ready and able to clearly articulate how your company's product is uniquely designed to solve their problem. Learn *why* people buy, not just *what* they buy. To begin your quest to become the best salesperson in your organization, read top sales resources like my friend Mike Weinberg's amazing books.

If you want to be future-proof, start seeing yourself as a revenue-generating member of the sales team. It's always nice to have sourced, or even closed, a few deals when it comes time to ask for a raise. There's nothing like directly impacting a revenue increase to improve your fellow team members' job security and support your case for a salary increase. Not to mention, when a recession hits and your company is forced to cut costs, they're going to think twice before letting go of a revenue generator.

To recap, here are four ways to future-proof your career:

1. Be an Early Adopter
2. Develop Your Emotional Intelligence
3. Look for (the Right) Problems and Suggest Solutions
4. Be a Revenue Generator

Your future is in your hands. You can wait until your company automates most of your job. Or you can creatively figure out how to use AI to automate the repetitive, manual processes you manage day in and day out. You can then gather real data on how much time and money you're saving your executive and company. Not to mention, you'll be freed up to focus on higher-value work.

Don't sit on your hands while the world moves forward. Embrace the future of work.

FIVE THINGS A ROBOT ASSISTANT CAN'T DO

I'm a practical guy who likes examples, so I thought I'd close this chapter with a list of five things robots will never be able to do for you—at least not at the same nuanced, intuitive level that you can.

- Run a meeting on your executive's behalf.
- Recognize that your executive is running out of steam and needs a few days off.
- Call a client, kindly explain to them how your company screwed up, and answer any questions they have.
- Give a genuine hug to a coworker who just lost their dog to cancer.
- Make an intuitive decision about which applicant to hire based on a five-minute, in-person interaction.

Do you want to position yourself amid the AI revolution? *Be more human.*

GAME-CHANGING QUESTIONS
FOR SELF-REFLECTION

Reflect on how future-proof you are by considering these questions:

- What problems have I identified at work that I could propose solutions for in the coming days?

- How have I developed my emotional intelligence?

- When was the last time I reacted instead of responding?

- Do I see myself as someone who can directly impact the bottom line? If not, why?

- Which manual processes can I automate in my work?

PILLAR 2

EMPLOY THE TACTICS

Leader Assistants employ the right tactics, to solve the right problems, at the right time.

Like many assistants, I was thrown into the role with little to no guidance. I was asked to schedule meetings, organize inboxes, and manage multiple to-do lists without any direction or examples to follow. I was usually told the "what," but rarely told the "why," and the "how" was always up to me to figure out.

In Pillar 2, we'll take a practical look at *how* Leader Assistants execute their work so you don't have to cross your glaciers alone. We'll spend most of this section focusing on tactics, because the tools you use don't matter if the tactics you employ are flawed.

Once you master these tactics, you can use whichever tools help you carry them out in the most efficient way possible.

These time-tested tactics will guide you throughout your career.

EIGHT

TIME MANAGEMENT

—

In today's fast-paced, busy-is-productive society, time management is a constant challenge. You're bombarded with texts, emails, meeting requests, shifting deadlines, employee conflicts, budget reviews, and...is your blood pressure rising yet?

You spend the majority of your day reacting to what's seemingly urgent, which leaves you little, if any, time or energy to work on what's actually important. You get to the end of the week and you don't know what you have or haven't accomplished. On top of managing your own workload, you "get" to manage your executive's time too. How are you supposed to get anything done?

The following five-step process will help you manage time like a confident, game-changing Leader Assistant.

STEP 1: EXAMINE

The first step is to examine how you spend your time at work. Time management starts with data, not feelings. What activities, tasks, and projects generally fill up your days? If it's checking email and booking travel, write it down. If it's grabbing coffee for your executive, document it. Don't just look at your calendar to see what you're scheduled to do next week. Track how you actually spend your time for three to four weeks so you have real data to work with.

STEP 2: EVALUATE

Now that you have a realistic picture of which activities get your time and attention, it's time to evaluate them.

First, identify the activities or projects that drain the life out of you. Which tasks do you avoid as long as possible? Which projects do you loathe?

Next, think through which activities or projects get you out of bed in the morning. Which tasks energize you? What part of your job makes you come alive?

STEP 3: ENVISION

Now think about where to focus your time and energy. If you don't know your goals—in work or life—you can't make informed decisions about what to prioritize. Here are some questions to ask yourself; they'll help you define success and identify your goals so you can more clearly envision your future:

- What's my definition of success?
- What are my top three goals at work for the next twelve months? Top three life goals?
- If I could do anything in the world, and money was not an issue, what would I do?

STEP 4: ELIMINATE

The key to time management is to regularly ask yourself this oft-forgotten question: *Should I spend time and energy on this project or task?* The following questions will help you determine which items to eliminate:

- Is this project or task in my job description?
  - If not, is it absolutely necessary for me to do my job?
  - If so, can I automate it or ask another team member to handle it?
- What long-term plan or goal does this project or task fall under?
- Why do I want to do this task or project?
  - Is this task crucial to the mission and vision of my executive and organization?
  - Do I simply want to look busy to my executive?
  - Is it because I don't have the courage to say no to my executive?

Think back to Step 2, when you identified activities that drain you. The above questions should help you discern whether you can eliminate a particular activity, task, or project. If you can't eliminate it altogether, the next step will help you delegate it.

STEP 5: EMPOWER

The final step is empowering your team—or someone outside of your team—to take the tasks you can't eliminate off your plate. Write down each task or project you'd like to delegate. Next, determine which person you're going to delegate it to. Then, set a deadline for when you're going to do it. In the next twenty-four hours, work to get a meeting scheduled with each person. The longer you wait, the less likely you are to take action.

It can be tempting to glaze over a process like this without engaging fully, but Leader Assistants take the time to work on their work. You can download a free in-depth worksheet to walk through the five steps at **leaderassistantbook.com/bonus**. I hope this process of examining, evaluating, envisioning, eliminating, and empowering helps you form a clearer idea of what you do with your time so you can manage it better.

NINE

TASK AND INTERRUPTION MANAGEMENT

———

An assistant becomes a leader when they proactively make decisions to address needs before they arise or matters continue to grow. A leader also continuously develops and refines processes to ensure the organization can work as efficiently as possible.

—JOLENE B., EXECUTIVE ASSISTANT (SEATTLE, WA)

Day in and day out we wake up to hundreds of them. No matter where we are, they find us and try to drain the life out of us. Some of us feel sick just thinking about them.

No, I'm not talking about zombies. I'm talking about interruptions. But the never-ending stream of text messages, emails, social media pings, and "Hey, do you have a minute?" taps on the shoulder can be as intimidating as a herd of zombies heading your way.

In the midst of these overwhelming days at work, I often get the feeling I'm back at home with my kids. You know when your kids pester you with nonstop requests like "Can I have a cookie?" or "Can we go outside?" It may as well be the coworker who stops by your desk four times before lunch with the classic "Does your executive have any availability this afternoon?"

My son Silas tries to get my attention.

Just think how many interruptions are waiting for you in the form of emails, notifications, or voicemails when you set this book down. (OK, maybe don't think about that right now.)

The truth is that assistants face more distractions and interruptions than most employees. In fact, one of the most common questions I get from assistants is "How can I manage constant interruptions?" Here are a few tactics for dealing with interruptions that I've gleaned in my time as an assistant.

MORNING ROUTINE

Leaders are intentional with their waking moments. If you don't plan (and stick to) your morning routine, you'll likely resort to a quick check of your email or other distractions at sunrise. Take a moment to write out a specific plan for your mornings in the form of a checklist.

Here's my ideal routine, as an example:

- Go to the bathroom.
- Brush my teeth.
- Eat breakfast with my family.
- Say goodbye to the boys before they head off to school.
- Shower.
- Get dressed.
- Pack my lunch.
- Grab a banana for the road.
- Head to work.

Your routine will change depending on your work schedule, kids' school schedules, weather and commute changes, and so on. This is totally understandable. Don't worry about being perfectly consistent. Simply commit to sticking with a routine for seven straight days, then take note of how your focus and productivity increase.

If you're not seeing results, give it another seven days. If you still don't achieve the change you want, try mixing up your routine until you find one that improves your focus. For instance, consider packing your lunch and choosing your outfit the night before to give you fewer things to remember in the morning, or add a fifteen-minute workout to really wake you up.

USE A SIMPLE TASK MANAGEMENT SYSTEM

Using a complex task management software, such as Trello, Asana, or Microsoft OneNote, can be a fun and productive way to track your to-do list. Nothing against those and other tools, but if you're not careful, you'll waste a ton of time deciding which tags to assign to each task, or how many subtasks to include.

Of course, your job as an assistant is to make sure nothing falls through the cracks, so you have to keep track of tasks somehow. I like to use a simple two-column spreadsheet and my email inbox to manage tasks. (I share more about these systems in chapters 11 and 12.)

In summary, I don't like to transfer tasks in my inbox to another tool. I prefer to save that time and manage those within my email. For tasks that come from outside of my email, I'll do one of two things: email the task to myself, or add it to my two-column spreadsheet.

Note: If you're part of a larger admin team or manage projects with several team members, you might need to utilize a more complex collaboration tool.

CREATE A SYSTEM FOR FILING INCOMING REQUESTS

Once you get your system set up, how you assimilate tasks into your system is critical. What do you do if a coworker swings by your desk or sends you an instant message asking for something? How should you handle these interruptions?

For me, 90 percent of the time I'll reply with "Can you please email me so I don't forget?" The rest of the time, I'll email myself (or write it on a sticky note) so I don't forget. The key is not to handle the request or even think about it in the moment unless it's very time sensitive. Instead, document it in such a way that you won't forget about it and can deal with it later.

Put the ball in your colleagues' court. Get used to saying, "Can you please email me?" Oftentimes, they'll figure it out without your help, or forget about it because it wasn't important. In other words, you'll never get an email from them. You're welcome.

TACKLE ONE TO-DO AT A TIME

In chapter 12, I talk about tackling your emails one at a time. This tactic also applies to your to-do list. Go to one task on your list, finish it, then move on to the next one.

If you're anything like me, you have one or two daunting tasks on your to-do list that you keep skipping over. (Read the last sentence again. You know it's true!) It's time to tackle these larger, time-consuming tasks. Block out some time this week to work on them until they're done. Game-changing Leader Assistants don't procrastinate.

SAY NO BY SAYING YES

When someone asks if your executive is available, the answer is not always a hard yes or no. Some of us want to say yes because we want to make people happy, but a Leader Assistant doesn't say yes to everything. Instead, be willing to say no to the unimportant so you can say yes to what is important.

In his book *Essentialism: The Disciplined Pursuit of Less*, Greg McKeown says it well:

> "Only once you give yourself permission to stop trying to do it all, to stop saying yes to everyone, can you make your highest contribution toward the things that really matter."

A way to say no in the moment without dismissing the needs of other team members is to say something like "Yes, I'm sure my executive would love to help, but I'll need to look into it and get back to you. Can you email me so I don't forget to follow up?" or "Yes, I'll look at their schedule to see if they can make it work."

These responses give you permission to look carefully at the request at a time when you can focus and not be concerned about disappointing someone on the spot.

Ways to say no firmly but kindly include "I appreciate you thinking of my executive, but he's not available at that time" or "Thank you for checking with me, but unfortunately they aren't available to help in this busy season."

One of the best ways to manage interruptions as a game-changing Leader Assistant is to learn to say no. In fact, I'm challenging you to say no one time this week, whether it's to someone asking for a meeting with your executive, a coworker asking for help, or your kid asking for a treat. Be kind, but decline at least one request. Set a reminder on your calendar every day this week if you have to. It's time to strengthen your "no" muscle.

TURN OFF NOTIFICATIONS

One of the best ways to deal with constant interruptions is to turn them off.

Set your phone to silent. Set your instant messaging software to "Away" or "Offline." Put a sign on your door that says "Do Not Disturb," or if you're in an open office, put your headphones on. You could even use a traffic light system. Red means "Don't interrupt me unless it's an absolute emergency." Yellow means "Think twice before coming in." Green means "Come on in, I would love to see you."

Whatever your "Do Not Disturb" system is, the key is to set time blocks each day for interruption-free times during which you set your status to "Away" for a couple of hours and get your stuff done! This could be the first and last hour of your day, plus your lunch hour—whatever works best for you to be productive. For example, I'm more productive in the morning and late afternoon, so I set my focus times accordingly.

INSTANT MESSAGES

Now for a note on the wonderful world of Slack, Microsoft Teams, or whatever instant messaging (IM) tool your company uses.

Bringing AOL Instant Messenger and the dreaded group text

message thread to the workplace might have been the worst idea ever. If you'd like to text a coworker a nonurgent question, IMs can be helpful—assuming they see your message before it gets buried or pushed aside when the next red dot pops up. When you want to be productive, however, the black hole of your chat application is the last place you'll find focus.

If your calendar had extended amounts of uninterrupted time, and you were disciplined enough to stick with your schedule, IMs wouldn't be so bad. The problem is, you miss the instant gratification and dopamine rush you get from each new chat message, so you constantly look for new messages. Game-changing assistants can't afford to be online and available all the time.

You can go along with the trend and tell yourself, "It is what it is," or you can take control of your IMs by applying the email and interruption tactics to those messages as well.

I'll let you in on a little secret of mine: I never set my IM status to "Available." Seriously. My name hasn't had a green "Available" dot next to it in years. Yet people still ping me for help, and I still help them—or I ask them to email me so I can help them later.

HIDE IN A DARK CLOSET

Sometimes the only thing you can do to avoid interruptions is to hide in a dark closet. OK, maybe not a dark closet, but sometimes you need to get away from everyone to get stuff done. You could work from home once or twice a month. You could book a conference room for the morning and lock yourself in it. You could spend half a day at a local coffee shop with your noise-canceling headphones on.

The point is to find an environment where you can focus, and where your team members won't be walking by you all day, tempted to ask you for help.

What's your quiet place? If you don't have one yet, find one this week and use it (and don't tell anyone about it). For me, it's at the office after everyone leaves. If I need to catch up on things or crank out a bigger project, I'll stay a couple of hours late one night to get caught up or work ahead. However, I'm careful not to make this a frequent occurrence, and when I do this, I'll often come in late the next morning to ensure I get enough rest.

IF ALL ELSE FAILS, USE PAPER

I do my best to have a positive attitude, but there are two things in life that get my complainer juices flowing without fail: paper and printers.

I can't stand having paper on my desk or getting paper in the mail. I prefer audiobooks over paperback. Typing is so much quicker than handwriting. Digital files are so much easier to edit, share, store, and search. I use my phone or computer to take notes. I sign documents with my computer. In other words, I save a ton of time working with digital files as opposed to paper.

Unfortunately, some industries (I won't name them because they know who they are) insist we print a document, sign it, then mail it with another printed document—or sometimes even require us to physically take the paper to an old, musty office building. Why can't they accept a digital signature? Do they hate trees? It's like they want to punish the world for moving on without them. I imagine them saying, "Take that, technologically advanced industries!"

Speaking of technological advances, or rather a lack thereof, let's talk about printers. They run out of ink, they jam, they don't connect to Wi-Fi, they print blank pages, and they leave streaks across your documents. Every once in a while, I can get a printer to print one page without fail.

With all the leaps in technology we've enjoyed over the past twenty-plus years, you'd think by now someone would've designed a printer that works at least 64 percent of the time. Nope. Instead, having to print something is the last thing any of us want to do with our limited time.

OK, where were we? Oh, right—tactics for managing interruptions.

As you can see, I have a disdain toward working with paper. Yet, I still use it. Not often, but I do use it.

I know, I'm a hypocrite, but there are times when my to-do list, calendar, and inbox are all so cluttered and jam-packed that glancing at them for ten seconds makes my head hurt. During moments like this, I'll grab one small piece of paper or a sticky note, set it next to my computer, and jot down a bulleted list of what I need to get done that day. In other words, I use paper when I'm overwhelmed. I use paper when I'm stuck. I use paper to help me get back to being productive.

Paper can also help me manage interruptions. When my executive stops by my desk to ask for something, I won't ask him to email it to me. I'll grab my pen and jot it down on a sticky note so I don't forget. So, yeah, paper and printers are terrible, but don't burn all your paper or smash all your printers just yet.

Do you have a small notebook or a sticky-note pad on your desk or very close? If not, get one there ASAP and have a pen close at all times. The next time you get bombarded with distractions in the middle of a big project, grab your sword (the pen) and your shield (the paper) and fight those distractions by writing them down and moving on.

TEN

CALENDAR

———

A Leader Assistant is keenly aware of the climate in the C-suite. They're ready to respond to shifts in scheduled events, fires that need to be extinguished, and challenges in scheduling meetings.

—PARIS D., EXECUTIVE ASSISTANT (MEMPHIS, TN)

I'm not a fan of assistants' "I do so much more than just schedule meetings all day!" battle cry. I know it's true, but I challenge you to think about it differently. Scheduling meetings is important, so take pride in your ability to manage your executive's calendar. After all, your executive's most valuable asset is their time, and you're tasked with managing that asset. (Feel free to add "Asset Manager" to your job description.)

How you manage your executive's calendar has a huge impact—positive or negative—on every aspect of their world. Their physical, emotional, and relational health. Their energy, productivity, and focus. Everything flows out of how they spend their time.

The problem is many assistants let others decide how their executive will spend their time. They passively wait for someone to request a meeting, then look for time on the calendar that might work. With an unstructured method like this, your executive's mind will wander while they're in meetings.

"Why am I here? How am I going to get through this? Shouldn't I be doing something else with my time? Will I ever eat again?"

As the meeting progresses, their inner dialogue continues.

"How did this happen? Did I think about my priorities when the invite hit my inbox? Well, not really."

"Did my assistant check with me before booking it? Probably, but it seemed important at the time."

"Did my assistant tell me I would regret taking this meeting, yet I ignored their warning? No comment."

HOW TO MANAGE YOUR EXECUTIVE'S CALENDAR BEFORE IT MANAGES YOU

Far too often, assistants and their executives let their calendars run wild. This leaves executives in draining meeting after draining meeting, dreaming of the work they could be accomplishing if only they weren't stuck there. It's a surefire way to ruin their productivity and suck the joy out of them, not to mention make them useless in meetings.

A calendar dictated by others turns into a burnout machine. It's time for you—the Leader Assistant—to take back the reins of your executive's calendar, managing it before it manages you. Take control so your executive can spend more time doing what they love, what they're good at, and what they're paid to do.

You can start by creating a rigorous vetting process to rank incoming meeting requests. Find out who your executive wants to meet with, who they don't want to meet with, and which VIPs should get bumped to the top of the list every time. When a request comes in, you can run it through your priority filter and act accordingly.

But having a vetting process isn't enough. With no structure to your executive's calendar, you might simply schedule meetings whenever they're free. Even worse, your executive might schedule them based on how they feel in that moment without considering how they'll feel when the time comes to attend that meeting.

When it comes to your schedule, no structure equals chaos.

THE IDEAL WEEK

To prevent RSVPs based on emotions, I like to set up an "Ideal Week" calendar.

I first heard of this concept from Michael Hyatt's blog and podcast. Hyatt credits Todd Duncan's *Time Traps* and Stephanie Winston's *The Organized Executive* for introducing him to the idea. With the Ideal Week tactic, you block out times on your executive's calendar for meetings, projects, checking email, working out, reading, taking breaks, and whatever else they want to spend time doing. It's a great way to set aside specific times each day for doing what they need to do, when they need to do it.

TIME	MONDAY	TUESDAY	WEDNESDAY	THURSDAY	FRIDAY	SATURDAY	SUNDAY
7:00 AM	Wake up	Wake up	Wake up	Wake up	Wake up	Sleep in	Wake up
7:30 AM	Workout	Take kids to school	Workout	Read	Workout		Time with kids
8:00 AM		Focus Block					
8:30 AM				Internal Team Meetings		Time with kids	
9:00 AM	Focus Block: Weekly planning (work from home)	Direct Reports	Focus Block: Projects		Focus Block: Brainstorming		Church
9:30 AM							
10:00 AM							
10:30 AM				Email			
11:00 AM	Check in w/Team	Check in w/Team	Check in w/Team		Check in w/Team	Lunch with friends	Family Brunch
11:30 AM	Weekly 1:1 with Assistant (Lunch)	1:1 Lunch Slot with a team member	Open Lunch Slot	Open Lunch Slot	1:1 Lunch Slot with a team member		
12:00 PM							
12:30 PM							
1:00 PM	Check in w/Team	Weekly Design Meetings	Phone calls	External Meetings	Email	Basketball	Nap
1:30 PM	Focus Block: Strategy (work from home)						
2:00 PM		Email	Weekly Sales Meetings			Focus Block	
2:30 PM							
3:00 PM				New Clients	Company-wide Meetings		
3:30 PM						Start 24-Hour "No Email" Break	Read
4:00 PM		Weekly 1:1 Coaching Call	Phone Calls/ Meetings		Wrap up the week	Family/ Friends	
4:30 PM							End 24-Hour "No Email" Break
5:00 PM		Dinner			Family Dinner		Family Dinner
5:30 PM	Email			Happy Hour/ Networking			
6:00 PM	Family Dinner		Family Dinner		Date Night		
6:30 PM				Family Dinner		Dinner/Date with friends	
7:00 PM		Personal Planning Night	Focus Block: Work Late at Office				
7:30 PM	Read			Family Night			
8:00 PM							TV/Movie Night
8:30 PM	Focus Block: To-Do List						
9:00 PM		Read					
9:30 PM				Read			
10:00 PM	Bed	Bed			Read		
10:30 PM			Bed	Bed			Bed
11:00 PM					Bed	Bed	

You can download the Ideal Week calendar template at
leaderassistant.com/idealweek.

For example, your executive might like to use their mornings to focus on projects, so adding an event called "Focus Time" on their calendar every morning from 8 a.m. to 10 a.m. could be a good start. Unless there's an emergency, you and your executive can agree not to schedule meetings during those blocks of time. (Quick Tip: Make sure you clearly define what a true emergency is to take out the guesswork.)

On the other hand, your executive might get their best work done in the afternoons, so you might schedule a 9 a.m. to 11 a.m. block on their calendar for "Meetings and Phone Calls." If this is the case, when you receive a meeting request, schedule it in the 9 a.m. to 11 a.m. slot, and leave your executive's afternoons open for focus blocks.

I've set up an Ideal Week calendar for my former executive, my current executive, and myself. It's an extremely helpful way for you—and your executive—to protect your time. Instead of allowing your calendar to be a blank slate that fills up as invites come in, your new schedule serves as a guide to direct invites into predetermined time slots.

With the Ideal Week, you're in control of your executive's schedule.

WHAT WOULD YOUR EXECUTIVE'S IDEAL WEEK LOOK LIKE?

If you have no clue how your executive's Ideal Week would look, take some time to audit their current calendar. Look at the big picture, as well as one meeting at a time, then help your executive consider the following questions:

- Is this meeting necessary?
- Does this type of meeting drain me?
- Does this type of meeting bring me joy?
- What time of day am I generally more productive?
- Am I dreading this meeting? Can someone else attend on my behalf?
- Does this meeting really need an hour, or could it be done in twenty or thirty minutes?

- What times and days of the week am I more pleasant to be around? (Hint: Schedule meetings at these times.)

As you work through your executive's calendar, you and your executive might determine a more extensive audit of their life is needed: their workload, their job description, and their goals—personal and professional. If so, I'd encourage you to walk them through my five-step process outlined in chapter 8 to help them do what they love and eliminate the rest.

Once your executive has a handle on how their current schedule is laid out, meet with them to discuss their preferences, then put together a first draft of their Ideal Week. You can create a new Google or Outlook calendar strictly for the purpose of crafting their Ideal Week, or you can use a whiteboard, a spreadsheet, or a Google Sheet to work it out first. Personally, I like to start with a Google Sheet. It's easy to quickly move things around, color-coordinate based on type of event, and share with my executive so he can make changes to it.

As soon as you get the Ideal Week close to a final version, overlay it with your executive's current calendar to see how far off it is. From this point, you can determine how long it might take to implement their new weekly rhythms. It might take a couple of months to completely switch over, but starting small is better than not starting.

Even after the Ideal Week is implemented, you'll tweak it here and there. As long as your changes are intentional steps toward more productivity and focus, that's OK.

ONE CALENDAR VS. MULTIPLE CALENDARS

Does your executive have more than one calendar? I know it might seem wise to split different types of events in your executive's life into separate calendars—maybe a personal calendar, a vacation calendar, and a work calendar, for example.

Generally speaking, especially in smaller companies or start-ups, I'm a big proponent of your executive having only one calendar. There's no reason to waste brainpower and endure decision fatigue by having to determine which calendar to use every time you create a new event. You can always use different colors or naming conventions to delineate types of events, but do it all on one calendar.

There's no work/life balance. There's only life balance. Your executive can't live two or three different lives—as much as they might like to.

TRACK YOUR EXECUTIVE'S TIME

The next game-changing tactic to add to your arsenal is time tracking—or auditing your executive's time.

In the business world, data is king. It's one thing to tell the board your executive spends too much time meeting with internal team members. It's another to show them a graph or chart with the exact number of internal meetings versus external meetings your executive had in Q1 versus Q2.

The data from the audit helps your executive stay honest about where they're spending their time, and allows them to reorder their priorities, if needed. Let's say your company hit its sales mark in Q1 when your executive spent 78 percent of their time in sales meetings. But your company missed its goal in Q2 when your executive spent only 24 percent of their time in sales meetings. Based on the data you gathered, the board might want to ensure your executive clears their calendar for sales meetings in Q3.

Tracking your executive's time is one of the more tangible ways you can impact your company's bottom line. Employ this tactic, and you'll further cement yourself as the revenue generator we discussed in chapter 7.

This tactic also helps you stay honest as you zoom out to look at how you've been managing your executive's time. It's easy to get stuck in the weeds as you schedule meeting after meeting, but when you look at data covering a six- or nine-month period, it can be eye-opening.

Did you give up on the Ideal Week tactic? Did you say yes to low-priority meetings that should *not* have made it on your executive's calendar? Sit down with your executive to review the data, talk about what's encouraging and what's not, and make an action plan for any changes to their schedule you need to make going forward.

I used to audit my executive's time manually. At the end of a quarter, I'd go week by week and count how many sales, internal, capital raise, networking, or other types of meetings took place. I would then report the numbers to my executive. Thankfully, there are now tools to automate much of this process, so I can audit my executive's calendar in a fraction of the time.

You can use a time-tracking tool, but many of these require your executive to trigger the tool every time they switch between tasks. I don't know about you, but my executives don't have the brainpower available to worry about something like this. You can also use a tool like Base's software for assistants (BaseHQ. com), which has an "Analyze" feature to track average meeting duration, who your executive met with the most, and more.

I've found the best system for my situation is a workflow using Google Calendar + Zapier + Google Sheets + Conditional Formatting + Manual Clean Up. When an event ends on my executive's calendar, Zapier creates a row in a Google Sheet and logs details from that event. The title, description, length, location, type, attendees, and date of the event are all added (Zapier allows you to customize which fields to include).

This system adds data from every single event my executive has to one spreadsheet. All I have to do is go back through and edit what's already there, set up a few formulas, and create some tables and charts to report an overview to my executive. This new workflow literally saves me days of manual work. If you'd like to see step-by-step instructions on how to set up this workflow, visit **leaderassistantbook.com/bonus**.

If you're not already gathering calendar data for your executive, now is the perfect time to start. Make it one of your goals during your annual review. Set aside time to research what tools will work best for you and your executive, and ask them what data they'd specifically like to track.

Employ these calendar tactics to better manage your executive's time—their most valuable asset.

ELEVEN

MEETINGS

———

It's not what your title is, it's how you influence others. From the greeting in the morning, to the phone call you answer, to the influence in a meeting—anyone can be a leader.

—ANGELA H., ADMINISTRATIVE ASSISTANT (PHOENIX, AZ)

I hate meetings. Long or short, food or no food, morning or afternoon—it doesn't matter. My definition of a meeting? When a group of unproductive people sit around a table with other unproductive people and discuss how they wish everyone else would be more productive. It's no wonder meetings drain the life out of this introvert.

Of course, there are appropriate times to gather people to make a decision. The problem is we like to schedule sixty-minute meetings with agendas that should take only ten or fifteen minutes to cover. But because we have sixty minutes allotted, we fill the time.

THE MOST IMPORTANT MEETING OF YOUR WEEK

I could go on about how meetings are a waste of time, and

why we should eliminate most of them, but I'll save that for another book.

As the Leader Assistant who books meetings, takes notes in meetings, and sends action items to attendees following said meetings, I'm willing to bet you share a similar disdain for meetings. But there is one crucial meeting that, if utilized well, can be the most productive meeting you'll ever have: *your meeting with your executive*. As much as meetings can be an energy-suck, this meeting is absolutely necessary. But it must be led well for it to be a game changer.

It's important to be on the same page with your executive. No one on your team can have a more positive—or negative—impact on their job than you. A regular, weekly meeting helps you stay productive, work together, and be strategic about what's ahead.

In an ideal scenario, meet with your executive for at least thirty minutes once a week. After a vacation or extended holiday, you may need to meet for one or two hours. Other weeks, you'll only need five to ten minutes. I recommend having this weekly meeting at the beginning of your work week, preferably on Mondays. This helps you and your executive prioritize what you're going to work on that week. Of course, every situation is unique. If Wednesday afternoons work better for you and your executive, have at it.

Ideally, this meeting will take place in person. That said, a phone or video call is OK from time to time (and it might have to be *all* the time if you're a remote/virtual assistant).

I also recommend you leave margin for a quick ten- to fifteen-minute call at the end of the week. It's a good idea to put these extra sync-ups on the calendar, even as optional, so your executive won't forget about them.

WHAT TO TALK ABOUT

One of the most painful workplace experiences is showing up to a meeting with no agenda. You can't let that happen when you meet with your executive, or anyone else, for that matter. In fact, *never schedule a meeting without an agenda.*

A simple way to build your meeting agenda is to ask your executive to email you agenda items as they come up. Don't reply to these emails, but compile the items into a list. Then, around twenty-four hours prior to the meeting, send the agenda to your executive.

When you meet, pull up the list and ask your executive about each item, one by one, in a rapid-fire manner. As they answer your questions, take notes on any pertinent details. Don't spend a lot of time on each item. Simply clarify *what* needs to be done, *who* is responsible for making it happen, and *when* it needs to be done, then move to the next item.

At the end of the meeting, or within twenty-four hours at the latest, send a list of specific action items and deadlines your executive needs to be aware of. Better yet, you can add these tasks to their calendar or task-management tool.

KEEP IT SIMPLE

There are hundreds of tools you can use to organize agenda items or meeting notes. Feel free to use whichever tool you and your executive prefer, as long as it's simple. By simple, I mean neither of you should spend more time organizing the agenda than it takes to complete what's on the agenda.

Personally, I prefer the simple, two-column Google Sheet I've used for several years with multiple executives. Here's what it looks like.

#	AGENDA ITEM	ACTION STEP(S)
1		
2		
3		
4		
5		
6		
7		

Get a copy of my template at **leaderassistant.com/agenda**.

It's simple but very effective. In the left column, I list the items I need to discuss with my executive. As I sit down to go through the agenda with them, I fill out the cell to the right of each item with very brief notes. These notes help me remember what my action items are when I go back through the list later. When the meeting is over, I have a clean and organized to-do list to tackle.

It's not rocket science, but that's OK. Don't overcomplicate something just to make yourself look smart. A game-changing Leader Assistant knows when to keep things simple.

Of course, you can lead your one-on-one meetings flawlessly but still not get anything done if your executive doesn't pay attention during the meeting. If it's a phone call, ask them not to scroll through Twitter or their inbox during the call. If it's in person, and they pull up their phone, ask them to put it in their pocket or turn it upside down. If they give you their full attention, not only will your meetings be more productive, but they'll be shorter. Odds are your executive will appreciate shorter meetings.

If you try this system for a few weeks, I'm confident you'll be more productive, and maybe even hate meetings less. Well, *this* meeting at least. However, you could implement your newfound meeting strategy and tool in other internal meetings your executive attends. In fact, if you require people to come to a meeting with an agenda, you'll often find many meetings have no agenda and are a waste of time.

THREE TRICKS TO MAKE SCHEDULING MEETINGS EASY

Have you ever thought about how you set up meetings for your executive, or do you just wing it? Do you find yourself in never-ending email threads trying to schedule a meeting?

After more than a decade as an executive assistant, I've come up with a few tricks for setting up meetings. These tricks will help you be efficient, helpful to others, and maintain control of your executive's calendar.

TRICK #1: MEETING BLOCKS

I spent time on the Ideal Week calendar in the previous chapter, but it's the foundation of scheduling meetings, so I'll mention it again. Block out times for meetings, and times for no meetings. One of the biggest benefits of creating and sticking with the meeting blocks and Ideal Week calendar strategy is your executive gets to decide when they want to have meetings—and when they don't. So before you move on to Trick #2, take some time to review chapter 10 and determine recurring, weekly times on your executive's calendar that you'll reserve for meetings.

TRICK #2: NEVER LET YOUR EXECUTIVE SCHEDULE MEETINGS

You know your executive's schedule like the back of your hand, so don't let your executive schedule meetings. They should trust you to set up meetings quickly and at times when they're actually able to make the meeting. If they try to schedule one, they'll likely double-book themselves or be tempted to book one at a time that doesn't align with their Ideal Week calendar. Lead your executive in this area by giving them templates to use when people reach out for meetings.

For example, if someone contacts them asking for a meeting, have them reply with the following (copying you, of course):

Hi [Recipient's Name],

I look forward to connecting.

+[Your Name] to schedule a phone call next week.

[Your Executive's Name]

If your executive doesn't want to meet with the other party anytime soon, they could say, "Copying my assistant to schedule a phone call next month."

Simple notes like this do two things. First, it sets clear expectations for the recipient so they have a rough idea of when to expect a meeting. Second, you get clarification on what type of meeting your executive wants with the other party: a phone call, in-person meeting, video conference, etc. It also tells you how urgent the meeting is: next week, tomorrow, or in a few weeks after things settle down, for example.

I love using this "code" to save the trouble of having to clarify at a later date or send additional emails. It also empowers your executive with language to use so they aren't tempted to schedule their own meetings.

TRICK #3: DON'T ASK THE OTHER PARTY TO SEND OPTIONS

When you make first contact with someone to set up a meeting, include a list of three to five dates and times that work for your executive. Of course, you should be able to easily find open slots because you've already added them to your executive's Ideal Week calendar (ahem).

You can also suggest a location in the initial email. On this note, gather a short list of places your executive likes to meet people for breakfast, coffee, lunch, happy hour, nice dinners, etc. That way you can schedule meetings at places your executive enjoys, and in parts of town they are OK commuting to.

Here's an example:

Hi [Recipient's Name],

[Your Executive's Name] is available to meet at one of the following times:

Mon., Oct. 11, 10 a.m.

Tue., Oct. 12, 9 a.m. or 3 p.m.

Tue., Oct. 19, 8:30 a.m. or 11:30 a.m. (Lunch)

Please let me know if any of the above times work for you, or feel free to suggest other times. [Your Executive's Name] can meet you at the Starbucks on Main Street, if that's convenient for you.

Thanks!

[Your Name]

Shouldn't you ask the other party to provide options? No. Unless the other person is on the top of your executive's VIP list, don't put the ball in their court.

Remember: You're helping your executive lead well and accomplish their goals without burning out. Don't give anyone the reins on your executive's time. Your executive wants you to take initiative because they have predetermined slots during each week that work best for meetings—times when they're energized and excited to meet with people, making their meetings more pleasant for all involved.

There's another reason to be so bold, and most people miss this. When the other party receives an email with dates, times, and a location already suggested, all they have to do is glance at their calendar to see what works, hit "Reply," and say, "October 19 at 8:30 a.m. at Starbucks is perfect, thanks!" This scenario keeps the email thread to no more than two to four emails.

On the other hand, if you send an email without dates or a location, the other party is forced to do all the work. They have to look at their calendar to come up with a few options that work for them. Next, they have to figure out a good location to meet—often without knowing where your executive likes to have meetings. When they finally send an email back with options, you're hoping they fit into your executive's predetermined meeting blocks. If they do, you reply with the option that works. If they don't, you're back to square one.

In this scenario, everyone ends up with at least two to three extra emails in the thread—or worse, your executive might end up going to a meeting at a time outside of their ideal meeting blocks, and at a location they don't like commuting to. So save the other person some time and energy by doing the work in the first email, and save your executive time and energy by maintaining control of their calendar.

TAKE CLEAN MINUTES

Taking clear and concise notes in meetings with fast-talkers, mumblers, and whiteboard-lovers is a challenging glacier to cross, for sure. As with most things in my life, I try to simplify minutes-taking by documenting two things for follow-up. First, I do my best to clearly write out a bulleted list of action items for each attendee, a summary of each item so they have some context, and the deadline for completion. Second, I always take pictures of the whiteboards to send with the minutes. Attendees, especially the visual learners, will appreciate being able to reference the intricate charts and other inspired scribbles as they work on their action items.

KNOW WHEN TO SPEAK AND WHEN TO STAY SILENT

One thing you've likely heard from speakers at conferences, on social media, or in blogs is the concept of taking—or grabbing—a seat at the table, because it's not going to be handed to you. I agree with this sentiment, but what happens once you have a seat at the table? How do you know when to speak up?

The first key is knowing what your role is in a given meeting. Are you there as a member of the leadership team? Are you there because your executive asked you to sit in and take notes? Are you there because you're managing the project the meeting is about?

For example, when I'm in a board meeting, I typically wear my "Support the CEO" hat and will take notes, make sure everyone has what they need, and chime in when I have data relevant to the conversation. I might hold back from sharing my opinions as freely in this context. When I'm in a leadership team meeting, I wear my "Direct Report to the CEO" hat. In this role, I'll be more active in the conversation and chime in with my opinions more freely. If it's a meeting about a project I'm managing, I'll wear my "Team Lead" hat and guide the conversation from the get-go.

Let me be clear on something: It's OK to play different roles in different meetings. In fact, Leader Assistants are aware of their role in each context, and act accordingly. In other words, you can't share your opinions about how one department is dragging the company down in the middle of a board meeting unless your opinions are based on data and relevant to the discussion at hand.

I'm not saying to sit in a corner, hands crossed, head down, and mouth shut. I'm saying, don't swing the pendulum so far that you lose control. Leader Assistants manage their tongue and control their emotions.

TWELVE

EMAIL

Email is the gateway drug of work; Slack is the crack.

—DAVID K., MY EXECUTIVE AND CEO (ST. LOUIS, MO)

The nonstop stream of text, images, attachments, sales pitches, and chain emails from Aunt Jackie can cause anyone to want to throw their laptop into a lake. Just thinking about how many unread emails you have sitting in your inbox while you read this is probably triggering some angst.

Have no fear, friend. I can help you manage the constant influx.

I've managed email accounts for several different executives over the years, in addition to several inboxes of my own. My experience has taught me a lot about how to manage email, but as you'll see in my "waking up to check emails addiction" example below, I still have plenty to learn. Of course, if I were to wait until I figure everything out, I'd never be able to help, so here are a few email tactics.

DON'T CHECK YOUR EMAIL FIRST THING IN THE MORNING

I hate to admit it, but I'm guilty of this far too often: As soon as I wake up in the morning, I grab my phone, check my email, and clear out my inbox. I convince myself that it's a productive way to start the day, but what if checking email first thing is actually counterproductive?

Sure, I might like the feeling of getting something done before I brush my teeth. But what's really getting done is *me*. In other words, the practice of checking email first thing in the morning isn't me taking control of my inbox—*it's my inbox taking control of me.*

Don't let your inbox seize the reins at the crack of dawn. Be disciplined about maintaining a morning routine that energizes you and keeps you focused on your goals for the day.

BLOCK OFF TIME TO CHECK EMAIL

If you check your email at all hours of the day, you feed an addictive "I need to check my email in case I miss something" cycle that distracts you from being productive. Dozens of times throughout the day, you refresh your phone to see if you have new emails. You could call it Email FOMO (fear of missing out).

To combat this, block off chunks of time in your week for checking email, then don't check email the rest of the time. Share your calendar with coworkers so they can see your "checking email" time blocks. This won't solve all your problems, but it can reset expectations with your coworkers as they see you aren't avoiding them; you're simply being intentional with your time.

ARCHIVE, DON'T DELETE

I know some people are afraid to archive emails, so they keep them in their inbox "just in case," but an inbox should be reserved for emails you still need to take action on. If no action is needed, get that mess outta there.

Unless your company has a policy requiring you to delete emails, archive them. With today's practically unlimited amount of email storage space, there's no reason to delete emails. Archiving gets emails out of sight and mind, but you can still search for them in the future if you need them, so archive, archive, archive.

FILTER, DON'T LABEL (MANUALLY)

Labeling emails seems like a great way to organize your inbox, but this tactic can weigh you down. You'll spend a ton of time and energy deciding which label to assign to a particular email, which will leave you with limited bandwidth to make important decisions. That said, labels can help you stay organized and on task, so what should you do?

I prefer setting up filters so when an email arrives, it automatically gets labeled. For example, any emails my executive sends me are automatically labeled with a bright blue "DK" (his initials). When I open my inbox, I can quickly spot emails from him. His emails are the number one priority in my job, so this label is very helpful. You can do this with other VIPs, as well as flight receipts or other emails you get regularly that can be sorted automatically. But don't go too crazy with automations and labels. Focus on auto-labeling the high-volume, repetitive emails.[2]

---

2   *I use Gmail for personal email and Google Suite for business email. Most email applications have similar features to the ones I discuss, just under different names.*

TACKLE YOUR INBOX ONE EMAIL AT A TIME

One way to knock out an insanely crowded inbox is to tackle one email at a time. If you find yourself overwhelmed as you look at the hundreds of emails in your inbox, home in on one email, knock it out, then move to the next one.

Don't go back to the list view of your inbox each time you reply to or archive an email. When you look at the entire list of emails, it can cause your head to spin and make it difficult to focus on any of them.

DON'T FEEL BAD FOR NOT REPLYING RIGHT AWAY

Personally, I like to reply to emails ASAP because assistants should strive to make responsiveness one of our key skills. That said, most emails in your inbox don't need a reply within twenty-four hours. If you tried to reply to each email as if it were equally important, you'd miss deadlines on items of higher importance.

If you don't reply to someone for a few days because you're busy focusing on more important tasks and emails, don't feel guilty. A friend of mine once said, "Voicemails are other people giving you work to do, that you didn't agree to." Emails are the same, so unless an immediate email response is part of your job description, don't sweat not replying for a day or two. This especially applies if you're sick or on vacation. Give yourself permission to not check email while away, and don't feel guilty about missing emails when you're out of the office.

THE "MARK AS UNREAD" TRICK

I have been using this trick for several years now. If an email in your inbox needs to be taken care of, mark it as unread. For example, if I read an email on my phone while I'm in line at the grocery store, but I don't have time to take care of what needs to be taken care of, I will tap the "Mark as Unread" option so I know it still needs my attention when I get back to my computer.

If you don't use a system similar to this, you risk forgetting to deal with key emails later. I learned long ago not to trust my memory.

SPLIT YOUR EMAILS BY TOPIC

Have you ever sent an email with a few questions to someone and they reply with an answer to some but not all of the questions? Frustrating, right?

People might overlook one of the time-sensitive pieces of information you request from them if the email is too long or covers too many different topics. They might reply to one of your questions but still need more time to review the other items. Because they sent a reply, they might think the email is taken care of. Then you never hear from them again.

If you need several unrelated decisions or pieces of information from someone, don't send one email with a long list of requests. Instead, *send a separate email for each request or topic*. This allows you and the recipient to deal with each request separately and makes it less likely that either of you will overlook something.

TACTICS FOR MANAGING YOUR EXECUTIVE'S INBOX

Despite the technological advances of spam and junk filters

today, dozens of pointless emails still reach your executive's inbox every day. Your company doesn't want to pay your executive to sift through junk emails. Additionally, even after you and the spam filters declutter your executive's inbox, the remaining emails don't necessarily need your executive's attention. There are some emails you can reply to quickly without consulting your executive. Other emails might be automated notifications your executive doesn't need to see. Still others might be information your executive needs, but not for a few weeks, and not in the form of an email sitting in their inbox.

Yes, managing your executive's inbox saves them time. But another big reason to do so is this: It will help you keep up with what's going on in the organization as well as what's on your executive's mind. You save time when you can check your executive's Sent folder to see if they sent that email they were supposed to send instead of bugging them about it. You learn more quickly when you can see how they reply to questions from potential clients. You keep up with the fast pace of your company when you're soaking up the same information your executive is.

Managing your executive's inbox gives you the opportunity to learn so much about communication, the industry your company is in, operations and management, and your executive's leadership style. You're more equipped to be a confident, game-changing Leader Assistant when you live inside your executive's inbox.

Now, some of you might not be able to get access to your executive's inbox because of a company-wide policy, or legal or security reasons. Or your executive might not want to give up the keys. If it's the latter, consider asking again, but keep the focus on how much time you'll save them. For more tips on having difficult conversations like this, check out chapter 21. Even if you know you can't get access, I still recommend reading this section. You can apply the tactics to other areas of your role.

Now that you're inspired to take ownership of your executive's inbox, here are a few things to remember.

CONFIDENTIALITY IS KEY

It requires a lot of trust for an executive to allow you access to their inbox. This should go without saying, but unless you come across something illegal, unethical, against company policy, or something that could be physically harmful to others, never share sensitive information found in their inbox. Don't share confidential information about the company at happy hour with your friends. Don't tell your neighbor about the pending IPO (initial public offering). You won't last long as an assistant if you can't maintain confidentiality.

AGREE ON A SYSTEM

When managing my executive's inbox, I won't archive an email if it's marked unread. I'll read it to see if I can handle it for him, but if I can't, I'll mark it as unread so he knows he needs to review it. Once I see that he's read the email I know it's probably OK to archive it. This is an effective system for keeping track of what he's seen already. However, sometimes it's not OK to archive an email if he needs to refer to it in a meeting the next day, or if it's one that requires more thought.

Over time, you'll get better at discerning which emails are OK to archive and which aren't. Of course, make sure your executive understands what will happen if they leave a message marked as read. In other words, agree on a system and clarify expectations to save you both headaches down the road.

Speaking of archiving emails, before our startup had a domain, my executive was using his personal email address. During one of our first days together, I noticed he had more than eleven thousand emails in his inbox, and thousands of them were unread. I brought it to his attention, and he commented on how he needed help. I quickly told him to select all emails in his inbox and hit the "Archive All" button. He nervously did and watched his inbox go from eleven thousand plus to zero. He immediately took a deep breath and said, "I feel like a new man!"

It can be intimidating to archive emails in your executive's inbox, especially if you're new to the process or new to your executive. Just remember: You're not deleting them. They can always be found later if needed. Archived emails aren't gone forever.

DRAFT ON BEHALF

Drafting an email on behalf of my executive is one of the highest-ROI (return on investment) activities I do.

Sometimes I know what the email needs to say, so I draft it and let him know it's ready to review and send. When I don't know what the email needs to include, but I know who my executive needs to follow up with, I can still save him time. I'll start a draft email to the recipient, include an intro and outro, leave the body blank, and let my executive know he needs to fill it in and send it. This saves him a few minutes finding the right email address. It also sits in his Drafts folder (which I have set up to always display at the bottom of his inbox so he sees it), ensuring he won't forget to take care of it.

PRIORITIZE EMAILS

Prioritize emails for your executive while sorting through their inbox. How you do it doesn't really matter as long as they can operate efficiently with whatever system you use. I use stars in Gmail (we're a Google Suite shop) to flag more time-sensitive or high-priority emails so my executive can more easily find them. As I mentioned earlier in this chapter, I also use automatic labeling for VIPs such as his wife, the board advisors, and his business partner. This way, with one glance, he can spot emails that have a higher chance of needing his attention in a timely manner.

NUANCE IS TOUGH FOR AI

It will take a long time for artificial intelligence to handle the nuances of human-to-human communication in email threads. An AI might respond perfectly to the content of an email but be unaware of the context surrounding that email. Perhaps the recipient was just diagnosed with cancer—an important point that wasn't considered in the copy of the email. Now your executive is seen as inconsiderate and insensitive.

Personally, I don't believe AI will ever have the ability to reply on behalf of your executive like you can. If you employ these important tactics when it comes to managing your executive's email, you'll be in a good place when the AI assistants come for your job.

THIRTEEN

TRAVEL

———

An assistant leads by being the eyes, ears, mouth, mind, and hands of the executive, and performing every task with confidence and integrity.

—LISA R., EXECUTIVE ASSISTANT (MOUNT LAUREL, NJ)

I'll be honest: I am not a fan of booking travel. It's not the task itself; it's that there are so many variables that could change plans at any moment. My executive could decide to leave a day early—or cancel the trip altogether. The airline might randomly change its flight schedule. A flight might be delayed for hours because of a flat tire. You know how it is.

In light of this, I thought I'd share a few travel tactics you can employ as a game-changing Leader Assistant.

TRAVEL TACTICS

First, always be less than two minutes away from your executive's travel info. You never know when you're going to get that dreaded "my flight was canceled" call. Do you know your executive's known traveler ID? Do you know their passport number? What about their Southwest Airlines Rapid Rewards number? Personally, I use Capacity's AI-powered knowledge base to quickly access this type of information when I need it. You could use a OneNote file, or a spreadsheet, or another tool—just as long as you can quickly access the information 24/7.

Second, have the phone number of a travel team on speed dial. Maybe it's a local travel agent, or a global corporate travel team. When you're in a bind, a travel agent can often do more than you can. Find a team who can help with your travel emergencies, no matter the time of day.

Third, be ready to make decisions on the fly. One day my executive was stuck at New York City's LaGuardia Airport (LGA) for six hours. His flight kept getting delayed, pushed back up, then delayed again. I was on the phone with hotels, airlines, a travel agent, my executive, and the organizers for an event in Minnesota the following morning (which my executive increasingly feared he would miss). On top of all this, Meg and our two boys were about to land in St. Louis when a storm hit, and they had to reroute to Indianapolis.

At one point, I was texting my executive, who said his flight was supposedly about to board, while simultaneously talking on the phone with the travel agent who finally found one hotel room for NYC that night (after two hours of searching). The travel agent asked me if I wanted the room for $600. If my executive's now-boarding flight were to actually take off, I would waste $600 of the company's money. However, if his flight was canceled, he wouldn't have a room for the night. I made the risky decision to release the room, and I hoped it was the right move. The travel agent was (understandably) not pleased.

My executive's plane sat on the tarmac for ninety minutes, but it finally took off. I had made the right decision that night. Of course, I've made the wrong decision plenty of other times, costing my company money. Being a leader is not about always making the right decisions. It's about not letting the fear of making a wrong decision stop you from being decisive.

Another key thing to remember regarding travel is your executive's security. If they're traveling internationally, keep an eye out for travel notices and warnings. Is a virus outbreak affecting an airport your executive is scheduled to fly through? Is news about a national security situation breaking while your executive is about to board a flight? Be aware of what's going on in the world so you can be ready to make adjustments if needed.

ITINERARIES

The last tactic I'll share deals with travel itineraries. Some executives like an extremely detailed, eleven-page itinerary to be printed out, placed in a nice binder, and handed to them on their way to the airport. Other executives simply want their flight number and hotel info on their calendar. Still others prefer to use a travel itinerary software like TripIt.

I used to add so many details to my executive's calendar when they were traveling. Then one day, I picked him up from the airport, and he mentioned his calendar app was malfunctioning. He couldn't even see the details I'd added. In other words, he did just fine with the basics. Find out what your executive prefers and do it. There's no sense wasting hours putting together a fancy itinerary your executive won't even look at.

In summary, when it comes to travel management for your

executive, have a team of people and software tools there to support you at all times, be ready to make decisions on the fly, and build itineraries your executive will actually use.

FOURTEEN

PROFESSIONAL DEVELOPMENT

—

A Leader Assistant has the ability to work as a strategic partner, learn the business, and be proactive and enthusiastic about improving their skills.

—MINA I., FREELANCE EXECUTIVE ASSISTANT AND
EVENT MANAGER (MELBOURNE, AUSTRALIA)

I love this quote from James Clear's *Atomic Habits: An Easy & Proven Way to Build Good Habits & Break Bad Ones* (a great book, by the way):

> "With outcome-based habits, the focus is on what you want to achieve. With identity-based habits, the focus is on who you wish to become."

Leaders look for ways to learn, grow, and improve in all areas of life and work. But understanding your motivation for professional development is important. The root of your desire to improve shouldn't be to achieve an outcome. Your motivation for improving should be to become, and own your identity as, a confident, game-changing Leader Assistant.

During the first eight years of my career as an assistant, I didn't have the right motivation. I was all about completing job tasks instead of becoming the leader my executive needed. I didn't seek out training, connect with other assistants, or own my development. I think I read two books in those eight years, and they were books my executive wrote…and the only reason I read them was because I was tasked with proofreading them.

I was so focused on taking care of my executive that I neglected my need for growth. The result of all this? I was underpaid, overworked, and eventually burned out. I wrote this book to help you avoid the same mistake. The second you think you don't have room to grow is the second you become replaceable.

Here are a few ways to own your professional development (because no one else will do it for you):

- Read books that help you with communication, self-awareness, emotional intelligence, and industry knowledge. Read the books your executive reads, too—and not just to proofread them!
- Take online courses and attend webinars and conferences dedicated to a variety of topics, both related and unrelated to the industry you're in. Don't just go to assistant training events. Go to events your executive attends as well.
- Connect with other assistants to learn a ton about how to lead in your role as an assistant. I'll talk about this more in chapter 20.

When I first sought out professional development, there weren't many resources for assistants. Thankfully, several great options are available today, so dive into the administrative professional training landscape and figure out what will help you the most.

To jump-start your research, check out **leaderassistantbook. com/bonus** for a list of helpful resources for assistants.

We'll walk through how to ask for training dollars in a minute. But first, be aware that investing in yourself doesn't have to involve a significant amount of money. Let's look at one of my favorite tactics for affordable professional development: being intentional with your daily commute.

DON'T WASTE YOUR COMMUTE

Whatever your mode of transportation, if you knew how much your commute costs you, would you value the time a bit more?

According to a *Bloomberg* analysis of US Census data, time spent on commuting amounted to an equivalent of $15,000 or more per year for cities like San Francisco and New York. Even if you don't live in one of the cities on the top of the list, you could be spending considerably on your daily commute.

How long is your commute? Are you wasting this precious time scrolling through social media on the train? Are you listening to a local radio station with mind-numbing advertisements blasting in your ear? Are you judging other drivers the entire way to work?

What would it look like to be intentional with your commute? You could listen to an audiobook or a podcast to learn how to become a better communicator. You could meditate in silence. Or maybe listening to talk radio, even with those annoying ads, is in fact the most effective way for you to decompress after a long day.

My commute is one of the few times I can listen to audiobooks and podcasts, or enjoy the alone time after a long day, without interruption. Whatever you choose, make good use of the time you have. Don't waste your commute.

PAID TRAINING

Affordable training is great, but every company should set aside training dollars for their assistants. It's common for C-suite executives, managers, and directors to attend expensive conferences, sign up for subscriptions to the *New York Times* or *Harvard Business Review*, buy business books, and even hire professional coaches—all on their company's dime. Meanwhile, one of the most critical team members in any organization—the assistant—often gets the short end of the professional-development funds stick.

Does your executive see how training you would greatly benefit *them*? Why won't your company set aside resources to equip and empower you?

Here are five likely reasons your company isn't paying for your professional development.

REASON #1: YOU DON'T ASK

When was the last time you asked for training dollars?

Waiting for your executive to call you into their office to say, "Here's $3,000 for you to go to that assistant conference next month. Have fun!" is not a good strategy. Instead, be assertive and put together a thoughtful proposal outlining what training event or course you'd like to participate in. Outline why you believe this training will make you better at your job and what specifically you're going to learn, and pledge to report back with a summary of key takeaways and action items after you complete the training.

Attach an itemized budget including travel expenses (if applicable) so your executive knows exactly how much money the training will cost the company, and how many days you'll be offline (if any). If your company has never paid for your professional development, ask if there's a designated budget for development or continuing education. If they say there's not, ask them if there's a different budget they could pull the funds from.

REASON #2: YOUR ASK IS TOO VAGUE

If your proposal covers all the bases, but the section detailing how it will help you be better at your job is too vague, your request will likely get shut down. You can't say, "I'll be a better assistant," and expect your executive to approve a $3,000 expense.

Instead, make the result of the training about them. For example, "This conference will teach me how to track key performance indicators (KPIs) for our company so we can have better data for making strategic decisions about the future. There's also a session on calendar management that will save me hours each week, freeing me to take these specific tasks off your plate going forward."

REASON #3: YOU ASK AT THE WRONG TIME

Timing is everything. If you present a compelling case for training, but right in the middle of a financially tough season for your company, don't be surprised if it's not approved. Be aware of the overall health and season of the organization before submitting a request. If your company just surpassed its sales targets for a third quarter in a row and they're handing out bonuses left and right, it's probably a great time to ask management to pay for your training. Another idea is to submit your request for training months in advance, with the hopes of getting added to the budget for next year. You likely can figure out when each department puts together their budget proposal and attempt to get your training dollars added during that process.

REASON #4: YOU ASK FOR TOO MUCH (INITIALLY)

You can aim high the first time you ask, but if they say no, come back with a smaller proposal. For example, if they say no to a $3,000 conference out of town, ask them for a $1,000 budget for an online course. Sometimes it's best to take what you can get, then document how much impact you had to the bottom line after your training. Proving the ROI for previous training will empower you to ask for more the next time. The ability to negotiate for more is a game-changing tactic we'll cover in the next chapter.

REASON #5: YOUR EXECUTIVE AND/OR COMPANY DOESN'T CARE ABOUT YOUR DEVELOPMENT

Finally, if you submit a strong proposal with a clear return on their investment, at a time when the company is thriving financially, you might still get shut down. If this happens, you're likely in an organization that doesn't value your professional development.

If this is you, have a conversation with your executive and HR manager. Let them know you would like their support as you seek to grow in your role. If you don't feel valued by the organization, tell them. Ask them why they won't provide training funds for you. This conversation will help you see whether they truly support you. If they don't, it's time to move on to a different executive and/or organization.

THE BOTTOM LINE

Unfortunately, some of you might have a difficult time finding another role at a company that will pay for your training. If this is you, it's time to get creative. Ask your executive if you could reallocate funds from another budget to pay for half of the training, and let them know you'll cover the other half out of pocket.

You could also contact the organizers of an upcoming event you want to attend and ask if there are opportunities to volunteer. Maybe you could run the registration table, which would give you the opportunity to meet other assistants, as well as sit in on most of the conference sessions.

If none of the above ideas work, you might have to pay for training yourself. If so, remember one of the best ways to invest in your future is to invest in yourself. Don't be afraid to spend your own money. We can't expect others to invest in us if we're not willing to invest in ourselves.

FIFTEEN

GOALS

WITH JILLIAN HUFNAGEL

———

To be a leader as an assistant, you have to be really great at what you do and always support the goals and objectives of your leader and the organization where you work.

—ANA C., EXECUTIVE ASSISTANT (TORONTO, ON)

Goal setting during annual performance reviews can be intimidating. Will you set goals you can't reach? Will you set goals that are too easy and show your executive you're not ambitious enough? What if your stretch goals distract you from getting your job done?

During my annual reviews, I used to stare into space and wish for the perfect goals to fall from the sky (they never did, by the way). Thankfully, I no longer hope for miracles during my reviews. Instead, I have tactics to come up with the right goals during my annual review—thanks to my friend, assistant advocate, and goal-setting guru, Jillian Hufnagel.

Jillian has supported executives in startup and established

companies across SaaS, healthcare, education, and security for more than seventeen years, so she has a unique and valuable vantage point on the topic of goal setting for assistants. Jillian graciously allowed me to share her tactics in the book, so get your highlighter ready if you want to become a goal-setting and goal-crushing Leader Assistant.

GOAL SETTING FOR LEADER ASSISTANTS (BY JILLIAN HUFNAGEL)

True Leader Assistants own their career development and know how to articulate their value to the organization.

Here are three keys to doing this:

1. Set the right goals.
2. Speak about your work using values-based language.
3. Master your physical presence and mindset.

1. SET THE RIGHT GOALS

For any employee, the *right* goals check these four boxes:

- They align with your organizations' mission, vision, and values.
- They map to the top-level strategic goals (objectives and key results, or "OKRs") of your organization.
- They're a little scary! True growth happens through discomfort. Your goals should challenge you beyond your day-to-day cat herding and fire extinguishing.
- They pass the SMART test:
  - **SPECIFIC:** Is it well defined, clear, and unambiguous?
  - **MEASURABLE:** Do you have specific criteria to measure your progress toward accomplishing the goal?

- ACHIEVABLE: Can you attain this, or is it impossible to achieve?
- REALISTIC: Is it realistic and relevant to your role, scope, and responsibilities?
- TIME-BASED: Did you clearly define the timeline to complete it?

If your goals check off the four boxes above, you're on a path to success. But don't forget: you need buy-in from your executive.

2. SPEAK ABOUT YOUR WORK USING VALUES-BASED LANGUAGE

It's critical to discuss your drafted goals with your executive to obtain buy-in on timelines, resources, and budgets, and to gain their commitment to support you where needed. Live discussion is always best so you can collaborate on adjustments to your goals in a healthy way. Let's practice how to talk about your hugely valuable work as you execute on your goals and prepare for your next one-on-one or review cycle.

As you're painfully aware, many of your managers and executives don't understand what you do all day—and they never will. Guess what? That's OK. They're not the assistant; that's your superpower. Let's look at a few ways you can articulate what it means to achieve your goals, so you can own your career development.

Keep the fine balance of being too vague vs. too granular.
Saying, "I just get things done," or "I always figure it out," is vague and devalues the impact you make. Worse, it can lessen people's perception of you. This is not how you own your career

development. On the flip side, being too granular will likely get you some head nodding, maybe a few eye rolls, or even glazed-over faces. Your leaders don't need to hear the seventeen steps it took to book a multileg international trip.

What they need to hear is the value you bring to the business—in terms they will understand.

An example of a goal—and how to talk to your executive about it.

Quarterly goal scenario:

> "Deepen my understanding of our company-wide initiative to increase overall customer satisfaction in our Asia-Pacific (APAC) region so I can best deploy my executive's time toward this goal."

How you talk to your executive about it:

> "Sarah, your trip to APAC is scheduled for March. Your detailed itineraries, visas, customer prereads, and trip postmortem are all in your calendar. Folder X also has all the documentation. You and I have time next week to review the itinerary in detail. As you know, better understanding our customer satisfaction program is an important personal growth goal for me this quarter. When you meet with the account managers to discuss each customer account for the trip, I intend to listen in on those. I will generate a list of any questions I have for you after the sessions to aid in my understanding of our program's success. I will also attend the trip postmortem so we can apply lessons learned to your next trip."

This scenario details the high value you bring to your executive and company, and reminds them you crushed every detail—

like you always do. You're owning your goal execution, sharing progress, and driving your executive to support you each step of the way.

Avoid the task-vs-outcome trap.

Tasks are "what" you did. An example of discussing a task sounds like this: "I organized the supply closet and secured a new break room vendor." Articulating the value of the task you accomplished sounds like this: "I increased efficiency and saved the department money by organizing the supply closet and securing a new vendor for break room service."

See the difference?

Be prepared and specific.

When in a one-on-one or review conversation, never ask, "How am I doing?" This question will likely lead to a generic response that's neither specific nor actionable. You'll each walk away feeling as if you just attended a pointless meeting.

Instead, be proactive. Arrive prepared with your list of goals and status to completion. You'll lead the conversation on roadblocks, delays, and successes. Call out what you're learning, observing, and how you're growing.

Don't hide, sugarcoat, or cover up the facts. Drive the conversation on gaps in execution due to lack of budget, resources, and time. Steer toward a solution by clearly stating what you'll need to get the goal back on track. Ask for specific support to get things unstuck.

But all of this can't be achieved if you're unable to show up in a professional and thoughtful way. Let's take a quick peek at what it looks and feels like to be in a highly effective discussion about your goals and development.

3. MASTER YOUR PHYSICAL PRESENCE AND MINDSET

The way you present yourself physically will help you feel confident and will invite respect from others. Sit tall, chin up, shoulders back, and arms open—even on phone calls. It might be awkward at first, but it works!

Control your body language, tone, and pace. Write out what you're going to say, and practice how you'll say it in front of a mirror or with a mentor. Say it a few times out loud to observe where you get stuck or tend to go off-topic.

If helpful, send your executive an email or document in advance outlining your goal progress. Ask them to review it and come ready to ask questions and share feedback.

You'll also need to master your emotions. Get your brain away from the epinephrine (a.k.a. adrenaline) loop of fight, flight, or freeze. Right before meeting with your leader, practice mindfulness, say a positive mantra, or try a quick meditation. Force yourself to slow down and take a deep breath.

Choose a room and seating arrangement that promotes face-to-face dialogue and open collaboration. Have a screen and whiteboard available, if needed. Bring in a stress ball, fidget spinner, Silly Putty, or whatever you need to keep yourself even-keeled. Ensure you have your executive's full attention, thank them for their support, and dive right into your list of accomplishments.

Be open to feedback and questions. Context and clarity can only enhance your ability to execute and drive toward the *right* goals and outcomes. *Ultimately, it's your career, and you have to own it.*

You now have tactics to set the right goals, speak about your work using values-based language, and master your physical presence and mindset. Go forth, crush goals, and lead well!

I trust Jillian's tips will be immensely helpful in your career. If you'd like to further explore the topic of goal setting, I've included links to Jillian's website, her LinkedIn account, and her free Goal Setting template at **leaderassistantbook.com/bonus**.

SIXTEEN

NEGOTIATION

WITH AL-HUSEIN MADHANY

—

A Leader Assistant is an individual who is courageous, empathetic, humble, and isn't afraid to lean into a challenge.

—ERIN B., EXECUTIVE ASSISTANT (MELBOURNE, AUSTRALIA)

This chapter is a snapshot of a very nuanced topic that could easily take up an entire book. It was co-authored with my friend Al-Husein Madhany. The contents of this section are based on proven salary negotiation strategies and tactics, specifically for administrative professionals and Leader Assistants.

These guidelines have helped me and hundreds of assistants make more money. Not to mention, the confidence gained from employing these tactics helps assistants negotiate with vendors and partners on behalf of their executives.

NEGOTIATE FOR THE MONEY YOU DESERVE

Two of the most frightening glaciers we experience in our professional careers are negotiating a starting salary and asking for a raise. As Leader Assistants, we are givers, not takers. We give, and we give, and we give. We lead from behind, and we make things happen from the shadows. We hope our hard work will be noticed and rewarded someday, but we feel we just have to wait for our turn. If we ask for more, we're taking away from someone more deserving than us—at least that's the story we tell ourselves.

The fact that it's uncomfortable to ask adds to our fear. It's not natural and it's not in our personality to ask. In fact, many of us were raised to believe we aren't *allowed* to ask for more. We were told if we take more than our share, we're being greedy. However, the truth is when we get paid more, it doesn't mean someone else gets less.

Asking is a proven silver bullet for increasing your salary. Al-Husein and I have seen this firsthand dozens of times. Long-time assistant advocates like Bonnie Low-Kramen and Phoenix Normand will tell you the same. But *how* do you ask?

Enter the business case: a written document you create that makes the case for your increased compensation so you don't have to do any of the talking. We'll go into more detail about the business case below, using Al-Husein's proven methodology that has earned assistants more than $1 million in compensation adjustments.

Compensation is another area of your career to own. Human Resources isn't handing out salary increases like candy on Halloween. Do you want a significant bump in pay? Ask for one. Even if you believe you're getting the highest compensation package possible, if you're a Leader Assistant who exceeds expectations on a regular basis, it's likely you can make more.

In fact, if you haven't received more than a cost-of-living adjustment in at least three years, you might not be getting paid market rate. It's time you take the reins back on your compensation and, ultimately, your career.

The counterintuitive part is your executive will respect you *more* if and when you negotiate for a raise. Why? They'll see you stand up for yourself during the process and be encouraged to know you'll use the same strategies to negotiate on their behalf.

Let's look at a few of these game-changing negotiation tactics you can employ as you ask for a salary or equity increase.

TAKE ADVANTAGE OF A GOOD ECONOMY

In a booming economy with a low unemployment rate, many assistants leave companies after only a year or two. Why? Because they can make significantly higher salaries if they move to a different company every couple of years versus staying at the same company for several years. Take advantage of a strong economy and negotiate for a raise—or find a higher-paying role elsewhere.

YOUR STRATEGY DEPENDS ON WHOM YOU TALK TO

If you're talking to the executive you work with day in and day out, your strategy must be different than if you're talking to the HR department. The context and relationship are key. For example, if you're talking to your executive of several years, don't treat it as a negotiation, but as a conversation. However, if you're talking with a hiring manager or external recruiter, you can stick to the business of negotiating.

NEVER ACCEPT A VERBAL OFFER

If you receive a verbal offer on the phone or in person, *do not accept it.* A verbal offer is not an offer. Ask them to put it in writing. Let them know you'll review the written offer and consult with your financial planner before responding.

BUILD A BUSINESS CASE

The best negotiation tactic is to build and present a business case to your executive and HR department so you can stay in the role you love, but make more money. Here's an outline of Al-Husein's six elements of a business case for assistants.

SIX ELEMENTS OF A BUSINESS CASE
1. COVER LETTER TO YOUR EXECUTIVE

Write a cover letter to your executive making it clear you love working for the company. Let them know you can't see yourself working anywhere else. Tell them you love the working relationship you have (if you do, of course. If you don't, find a different job). Remind them you're a Leader Assistant, culture carrier, and brand ambassador. You embody your company's values. Be sure to illustrate how.

Identify why you deserve a raise and are being undercompensated. Here are a few reasons you could provide:

- Because of the increasing number of responsibilities you've taken on during the past X number of years as per your attached job description, kudos, and performance reviews.
- Because you're currently below market rate. Provide data to show this. Note: Sometimes the best data you can get will

come from asking other assistants, or even interviewing for other positions, in your area.

- You've executed your responsibilities in the midst of a demanding, fast-paced environment. (Don't ask for a raise if you did not meet or exceed expectations in the previous half of the year.)

2. DESCRIPTION OF THE JOB YOU WERE HIRED INTO

Include a copy of your original job description. If you never received one, you could include a copy of the job posting you applied for, or the offer letter you received.

3. DESCRIPTION OF THE JOB YOU'RE DOING TODAY

Make a copy of your original job description. Add all the additional responsibilities you've taken on. Use a different color of text so it's clear how much your current job description has evolved from your original one.

4. YOUR UPDATED AND CURRENT RESUME

Including a copy of your updated resume will not only remind your executive how qualified you are for the job, but it will show them how ready you are for the open job market, if needed.

5. KUDOS OR ACCOLADES YOU'VE RECEIVED DURING YOUR TIME AT THE COMPANY

Did a coworker thank you for your excellent work on a project via email or IM? Screenshot it and include it. You can also include documented performance reviews as an addendum.

6. ATTACH MARKET DATA YOU'VE RECEIVED REGARDING ASSISTANT SALARIES

This data can come from assistants in your area, a job offer you received, intel from recruiters or a career coach, or compensation studies. Visit **leaderassistantbook.com/bonus** for a list of salary surveys.

Once you've built your business case, be sure to include the following in the email you attach the business case to:

- You love working at the company, don't want to work anywhere else, and are excited about the future together.
- You're asking for a raise. You believe you're being undercompensated based on current market rate and your updated job description.
- You're ready to speak with them about this when they're available. If it's your executive, let them know you've put time on their calendar to have this conversation.

LEVELS AND TITLES

In many companies, your title plays a major role in determining the salary band you fall into. Particularly if you work for a large company with lots of levels, you'll want to include a proposal for a title change within your business case. If you're not sure what your company's career path is for assistants, ask HR. If they don't have one, do some research and create one yourself. Check out **leaderassistantbook.com/bonus** for much more on the topic of levels and titles for administrative professionals.

Again, no one cares about your future as much as you do, so you've got to take ownership of your career.

SEVENTEEN

THE PERFECT RESUME

WITH AL-HUSEIN MADHANY

———

To be honest, I've never had to submit a resume. I've always landed my jobs through people I know. When I was between my current and previous jobs, I put together a very professional resume, but I ended up not even using it for my current role. I've hired assistants and reviewed hundreds of resumes in my role, however, so I do know enough to be dangerous.

That said, similar to the Goals and Negotiation chapters, I'm going to invite an expert on the subject to help me out. My friend Al-Husein's resume tactics work wonders for assistants and administrative professionals, and I'm excited to share an overview of his methods with you in this co-authored chapter.

THE PURPOSE OF YOUR RESUME

Most people think the purpose of a resume is to get a job. That's not true. The sole purpose of your resume is to pique the interest of a recruiter or hiring manager in about six seconds—just long enough for them to pluck it out of a pile and *want* to schedule an initial phone screen with you. Your resume will *not* get you a job or help you get to a second interview.

Your resume is an 8.5-by-11-inch piece of paper that recruiters force you to use as a means of *marketing* yourself to them. No emojis. No gifs. Not even color. Just black and white. Period. How are you supposed to stand out in a crowded marketplace in which everyone's resumes look so similar? Again, your resume will be reviewed for an average of six seconds—assuming a human even sees it.

More and more companies use machine learning in high-volume recruiting for roles like software engineers and executive assistants. The applicant tracking system feeds your resume into a machine that spits out a number based on trigger words and how closely the words on your resume match the core job description. The higher the number, the more likely your resume will make it in front of a human for a quick review. It can be harder to get a job at some companies than it is to get into Harvard University, so how do you stand a chance of getting your resume seen? How can you make your resume pop?

You've got to make your resume memorable to properly market yourself to the recruiter who grants you seconds of their attention. The following core tenets and sections of a resume are based on tactics that Al-Husein has employed for hundreds of administrative professionals. These assistants used this resume methodology to successfully land phone screens that led to life- and career-changing jobs.

First, let's review the five core tenets of a memorable resume.

FIVE CORE TENETS OF A RESUME

TENET 1: NO MISTAKES

The first key is to double-, triple-, and quadruple-check for typos, poor punctuation, incorrect dates, and other errors. Have a few friends or a coach review your resume to be safe. Assistants are expected to be detail-oriented and can't afford to make mistakes. If a recruiter sees a mistake on your resume, you're toast.

TENET 2: LESS IS MORE

Keep your resume to no more than one page long. Remember: Your resume will be reviewed for just six seconds. If it's one page, you have a higher chance of the recruiter seeing the important parts. Also, make sure there's lots of white space. Don't cram it all in. Rather, leave most of it out.

TENET 3: LIMITED FORMATTING AND INTENTIONAL BOLDING

You want to use some formatting to highlight interesting and important tidbits; just don't go crazy with it. But do be intentional about your bolding. For example, if you managed a budget of $1 million in one of your roles, you definitely want to bold that piece of information and *not* the education section of your resume.

TENET 4: METRICS (IF YOU CAN'T MEASURE IT, IT DOESN'T MATTER)

Executives love data, so be sure to include things you can measure. For example, if you led a team of five assistants, include that. If you supported a project that helped increase your company's revenue by 15 percent, include that as well. Were you responsible for saving the company money through the processes you set up and deployed? Measure it, then bold it. On your resume, lead with data, not drama.

TENET 5: MACHINE LEARNING COMPLIANT

Many companies use software to scan resumes initially, so your resume needs to stand out to machines too. If you're applying for a role and the job description includes project management as a key element, be sure to include the term "project management" in a prominent way on your resume. If a role you're interested in has the term "jack of all trades" in the role description, adapt your resume accordingly. In fact, submit a different resume for every job you apply for. Yes, *every* job. Why? Because your resume must reflect the details of the job description, and each job description is different.

SEVEN SECTIONS OF A RESUME

Now that you know the core tenets, let's review the seven sections to include on your resume.

SECTION 1: WHO YOU ARE

Include your name, city, phone number, email, and entire LinkedIn URL. Your name should *not* be the largest font on the page. Why? Because your name isn't memorable. You're a stranger to the recruiter and likely always will be. As for your email, don't use a Yahoo or Hotmail email address. Use a Gmail or Outlook email instead. If you don't have one, create one.

Don't include your address. Your city should be the city of the job you're applying for. For example, if you live in San Diego, but you're applying for a job in Silicon Valley and would like to relocate there, put Silicon Valley down as your city. Again, the purpose of your resume is to get the phone screen. If you list San Diego on an application for a job in Silicon Valley, your odds of landing an interview dramatically decrease. You can explain to them on the call that you live in San Diego but are willing to relocate. A resume is not the place to explain this.

SECTION 2: WHO YOU ARE IN THE WORKPLACE

This is where you use large font. List three or four attributes, in big words, underneath your bio data section—things like "chaos tamer" or "project manager," for example. Choose phrases that describe what you will do for the executive, should they choose to hire you.

SECTION 3: CORE SKILL SET

This is where you regurgitate what's on the job description you're applying for. If the role responsibilities include descriptors like resilient, diplomatic, or tech savvy, include them in your core skill set section, and selectively bold them.

SECTION 4: LEAD WITH IMPACT

This section is for you to list anything notable you've achieved in your career that might differentiate you from others. Again, you can bold select phrases throughout, but don't go overboard with formatting.

SECTION 5: RELEVANT EXPERIENCE

In this section, briefly list your professional experience, if relevant. For example, unless you're applying to be Executive Assistant to the CEO of Taco Bell, you don't need to waste ink letting them know you ran the Taco Bell drive-thru window in college. In general, don't take more than two or three inches of space, and do your best to stick to one line per role.

SECTION 6: EDUCATION

In this section, list the certifications, education, or specific training you've received. Don't list everything, and make it short and sweet. It's preferable not to include graduation dates.

SECTION 7: PASSIONS

This section is not for you to list your hobbies. Instead, include a couple of your *passions*. In one word, or via a short phrase, talk about what you love. Show them you're a human too. For example, if you know the recruiter or executive you're applying with loves dogs—and you do as well—then list dogs as a passion. Be transparent about who you are as a person, but communicate it via tight, pithy wording.

GO DEEPER

The above tactics from Al-Husein will help you craft a perfect resume, which is a key part of being a game-changing Leader Assistant.

I know you're probably itching for more, but this is all the room I have in this book. The good news is Al-Husein and I put together an in-depth online course on the topic of resumes for assistants. Visit **resume.assistantsguide.com** to enroll.

EIGHTEEN

COMMUNICATION

———

*Leader Assistants are strategic business partners to their execu-
tives and hold positions of knowledge and empathy. The ability to
communicate across all levels of a business is key, and an assistant
has to know how to blend in and act differently depending on
what's called on them in their role.*

—JENNIFER W., FOUNDER AND DIRECTOR

(OXFORD, UNITED KINGDOM)

Your ability to communicate with your executive has a huge
impact on how well you work together. I discuss your direct
relationship with your executive in chapter 21, but first I want
to share a few general communication tactics. Some of these
might seem basic to you, and that's OK. I'm sharing them here
because I'm shocked at how often I come across poor communication in the workplace.

WRITTEN

Avoid typos and poor formatting in your written communication. If you have to send a long email with a bunch of items,
please spare us all from the extremely long paragraph with a

bunch of hidden action items throughout. Use bullets, headers, bold formatting, and even color text if necessary.

Also, don't hit "Send" on an email until you've reread it at least once or twice. I've been in situations where employees didn't respect certain coworkers because of poor written communication skills. In this day and age of emails, don't let someone's first impression of you, your executive, or your company be tainted by a misspelled word or an email addressed to the wrong person.

VERBAL

As an introvert, I'm not a fan of phone calls. Most of the time, I prefer to email or text. However, over the years, I've had to get over my personal preference and become a professional phone-call maker and taker. When on the phone, be sure to enunciate, be kind to whomever you're on the line with, and remember to get the information you need so you don't have to call back.

Another note about verbal communication in the workplace: Project your voice in a clear and confident way so people can hear you—especially if you're on a conference call. There's nothing worse than sharing a profound insight, only to have someone respond, "I couldn't hear any of that. Could you repeat it, please?"

NONVERBAL

This section is a good reminder for me, as I forget about non-verbal communication far too often. When you're in meetings, don't sit slouched, with your eyes on the table and your hands crossed. When you're talking to coworkers in the break room, smile and look them in the eyes. When you're watching someone give a presentation, stay alert and show them you're interested.

KNOW YOUR STYLE

Bestselling author and leadership coach Mark Murphy says we fall into one of the following communication styles: Analytical, Intuitive, Functional, and Personal. You can take a free assessment on his website to help you determine which of the four communication styles you most frequently use. You can find a link to the assessment at **leaderassistantbook. com/bonus**.

Here's a quick summary of the four styles of communication:

- **Analytical** communicators like hard data, real numbers, and are suspicious of people who make decisions without data to back them up.
- **Intuitive** communicators like the big picture, avoid the details, and cut right to the chase.
- **Functional** communicators like processes, timelines, and step-by-step plans.
- **Personal** communicators value and use emotional language and connection to discover what people are really thinking.

My communication style is Analytical, but my executive's style is Intuitive. He appreciates data, but he doesn't want to get bogged down in the details. So when I communicate with him, I do my best to keep things at a high level, and I cut right to the chase.

The downside to my Analytical style is that I'm often accused of being emotionally dead inside. I'll share more about my emotional life in the next chapter, but it's helpful to acknowledge that my lack of emotion can hinder my ability to connect with people who have a Personal communication style.

Explore what your communication style is, and figure out your executive's style. This will allow you to better understand where they're coming from, which will help you be more empathetic and adapt your communication to them.

PRIORITY-RANK YOUR METHODS OF COMMUNICATION

Another communication tactic for you and your executive to employ is to priority-rank your methods of communication so you don't treat everything as urgent. Clarify your executive's expectations for communicating via text, email, instant messaging, or phone. For example, you can use emails for nonurgent matters and save phone calls for very urgent matters.

I've been doing this for a few years now, and it has been extremely helpful. If my executive calls me, I know to drop everything and answer the phone right away. We're on the same page about this. He knows not to call me unless it's time-sensitive, and I know if he's calling me, it must be time-sensitive.

Here is how we rank our methods of communication:

- **Phone call:** Drop everything and answer it. Phone calls are an option on the weekends in case of emergency.
- **Text:** Review it ASAP and reply within a couple of minutes. Text is an option on the weekends in case of emergency.
- **Instant message (via Slack):** Review it ASAP and reply within fifteen minutes. I'm offline on the weekends, so

instant message is not a good option for my executive if he wants to get a hold of me.

- **Email:** Review it the same day, and make an informed decision on the timing of my reply. I'm not in my email on the weekends, so email is not a weekend communication option.

Feel free to tweak this system to whatever works best for you, of course, but whatever you do, get on the same page with your executive. This tactic of communication is a great segue to Pillar 3, which deals with relationships. After all, most relationship issues stem from a failure to communicate.

PILLAR 3

ENGAGE IN RELATIONSHIPS

Leader Assistants seek out and engage in relationships.

You've probably heard the saying, "It's lonely at the top." It means it's tough to make friends when you're in a position of power, and it's typically used when referring to CEOs, presidents, pastors, etc. A quick Google search tells me the saying originated from a Chinese proverb that literally means "It's cold at the top (of a mountain)." Feel free to fact-check this and send me an email if I'm wrong.

The point is your executive has one of the loneliest jobs. But you—the assistant who works side by side with them—also have one of the loneliest jobs. It's cold at the top for you too.

In my last role, I worked out of the founder's home office most days. Just me and his dog hanging out by ourselves. In my current role, I'm in an open office with ninety-plus team members, but I'm the only assistant, so it still can be lonely. Those times when you overhear a coworker plan a team outing while your team (or lack thereof) is comprised of you and your laptop. Or when it's performance-review season and your executive forgets to sit down with you to go over your evaluation. Or the countless times you're the last one at the office working on a project.

I experienced numerous moments of isolation, but I didn't truly grasp how lonely the role of an assistant was until I left my last job. After submitting my resignation, I was left with my family and a couple of close friends. I was on the outside looking in and struggled to process the emotions I felt. Sure, a lot of people knew of me—this comes with the territory when you're assistant to a founder. But very few people truly *knew* me.

I still run into people around St. Louis who I thought were part of my community back then. I'm quickly reminded of my isolation when they say things like "Are you back in St. Louis? I thought you moved to Kansas City." Nope. I've been in St. Louis this entire time, friend.

One of my all-time favorite TV series is a show called *Rectify*. The main character spends nearly twenty years on death row before a new DNA test nullifies his conviction and he's released. I was watching one episode while still in the thick of trying to rectify (pun intended) my loneliness. This quote from the main character hit a bit too close to home for me:

> "When you are alone with yourself all the time, with no one but yourself, you begin to go deeper and deeper into yourself until you lose yourself. It's a perverse contradiction. It's like your ego begins to disintegrate until you have no ego. Not in the sense that you become humble or gain some kind of perspective, but that you literally lose your sense of self. And I'm not sure anyone, unless they have gone through it, can truly understand how profound that loss is."

I know my situation was nothing compared to being on death row for twenty years. And my lack of connection to others was partly my fault for giving up on people (more on this later). But this quote describes exactly how I felt at the time. I had lost my sense of self in the midst of serving others. I was disconnected from those who could understand what I was going through. If I was going to cross that glacier, I was going to have to do it alone.

We'll dive into how you can avoid ending up alone like I was in the coming chapters. But first, let's look at one of the biggest contributors to my isolation: the dehumanizing nature of being an assistant.

NINETEEN

THE DEHUMANIZATION OF ASSISTANTS

———

We've all been there. Someone across the room waves in your direction. You wave back, but then you quickly realize they weren't waving at you. You pretend you were waving at someone else so you don't look like a fool.

A similar scenario happened to me over and over again during my time as an assistant at my last organization. I'd walk into a room and someone would come up to me and say hi. I'd say hi back and we'd exchange small talk. As the conversation progressed, I'd realize this person wasn't ultimately interested in me. This was a common conversation for me:

"How's your boss doing?"

"He's good. Things are crazy busy as usual, but he's hanging in there."

"Good, good. (Awkward pause.) Well, let him know I'm thinking about him and tell him if he ever needs anything to give me a call."

"Sure thing. Thanks a lot!"

On one hand, I saw these frequent interactions as just part of the job. However, they didn't just happen at work. They occurred "off the clock" in social settings, during random run-ins at the grocery store, via text messages, and more.

Deep down, I know my value as a human being doesn't come from other people. However, when the people I interacted with continued to look through me and at my executive, it took a toll. It was dehumanizing. I felt like a tool that others used to get the inside scoop on my executive. I felt less like a valuable human and more like a robot.

I eventually gave up trying to relate to people as friends of mine, and instead related to almost everyone as friends of my executive. I stopped opening up and being vulnerable with others. I assumed anyone who tried to get close to me just wanted to use me to get to my executive. I thought the dehumanizing experiences I had as an assistant were just the way the world is. It became difficult to believe the best about people, and it still is to this day.

PEOPLE ARE DRAWN TO POWER

People like to befriend those in power more than those supporting the ones in power. They want to be in these "power relationships" to make themselves feel important. Once you're aware of someone's motives, it's no longer surprising when they get close to you to get close to your executive. But it's still dehumanizing.

It has been years since I left my previous organization, and I can count on one hand the number of people who've reached out along the way to see how I was doing. All the while, dozens upon dozens reached out to my previous executive (who was fired) to check in on him. People are drawn to those in power, even when the powerful fall.

Of course, executives also contribute to the dehumanization of assistants. One assistant told me their executive walked by their desk every day for years but rarely acknowledged their presence and never even learned their name. Countless more assistants have shared their stories of disrespectful and abusive executives, as well as hostile work environments.

What about you? Do people try to get close to you just to get close to your executive? Do your "friends" change based on whom you're supporting? Do coworkers introduce guests to your executive but not to you? Is your executive abusive? To engage in relationships in a professional and helpful way, first acknowledge where you've experienced dehumanizing relationships.

VULNERABILITY

When I was a teenager, I was emotionally aware and willing to be vulnerable. At the time, I thought it was great to be the guy the girls could rely on. These female friends would tell me everything as we chatted on AOL Instant Messenger at all hours of the night. I fell in love with a few of them (I bet you saw this coming) and shared how I felt.

Time after time, I'd get the dreaded response: "Jeremy, that's sweet, but you're like a brother to me." I'd be crushed.

I repeatedly fell in love with people who didn't share my sentiment. Eventually, I chose to avoid the pain involved with being so vulnerable and started to close myself off emotionally.

I then found out my dad had an emotional affair, which affirmed and amplified my newfound reluctance toward vulnerability. I was well on my way to shutting down emotionally, and all of this was *before* the dehumanizing relationships I experienced as an assistant.

Over time, I didn't simply stop being vulnerable with people—I began to neglect and avoid relationships altogether. I convinced myself I didn't need people. At the time of my career shakeup, I was connected to just one assistant whom I could call.

I've since connected with other assistants who've been through what I've been through. This has been refreshing and encouraging as I attempt to rebuild my relationship capacity, one conversation at a time. I'm much less cynical and cold-hearted than I was before, and although I still keep things close to my chest for a long time, I'm at least aware of the struggle.

On one hand, I want to encourage you to be vulnerable and open up to others. As Alfred Lord Tennyson put it, "'Tis better to have loved and lost than never to have loved at all," right? On the other hand, I want to tell you not to trust anyone and to go it alone. I'm not going to do that, though, because I now know that's a miserable way to live.

Instead, I'll encourage you to be vulnerable, take risks, and put yourself out there, but also to be aware of how people might use or abuse you. Life is too short to journey across glaciers alone, but it's also too short to let others walk over you to climb their own glacier. Take an audit of your current relationships, then do your best to limit the time spent with those who use you. If you're not sure which of your relationships are healthy, find a trusted friend with an outside perspective to help.

Hopefully, you haven't experienced many dehumanizing interactions in your career, but if you have, please don't shut down. See a counselor or therapist like I did. Hire a personal development or career coach. Take calculated risks. Be vulnerable—before you're stuck without anyone to be vulnerable with.

In the rest of Pillar 3, we'll look at growing your network of assistants, then walk through ways to lead your relationships with your executive and your coworkers.

TWENTY

NETWORKING

———

No one, not even your best friend, has the ability to understand what we (assistants) go through.

—MONIQUE HELSTROM

Similar to how a mountain-trail guide won't know what it's like to be on a glacier unless they've been on one, the only group of people on the planet who truly get what assistants go through are other assistants. Your executive and coworkers won't understand at a deep level, and you'll likely change executives, coworkers, and companies throughout your career. However, a strong network of assistants will stick with you through the good, the bad, and the ugly. Not to mention, your network of assistants will often help you land your next job.

To remedy the isolation and loneliness I felt in the middle of my career glacier, I reached out to assistants on LinkedIn, Slack, Facebook, Twitter, you name it—anywhere I could find assistants to connect with. I networked until I couldn't network anymore. I began to ask for advice, share tips, and exchange stories with assistants from Boston and Omaha to South Africa and Australia.

As my LinkedIn network continued to thrive, more doors opened. I was recruited for senior executive assistant roles at companies such as Facebook and Amazon. I flew across the world to train assistants in Germany, Hong Kong, and Thailand—and got paid to do so.

GROW YOUR NETWORK (BEFORE YOU NEED IT)

Don't get stuck on a glacier with nowhere to turn. Instead, grow your network so you have one when you need it. Add value to LinkedIn, Slack, and Facebook communities. Go to local assistant meetups or conferences. If there aren't local events, start an assistant happy hour or a "lunch and learn." Ask other assistants to grab coffee, or hop on a video call to share your happies and crappies from your week. (Oops, I mean highs and lows—happies and crappies are what we do with our boys at the dinner table.)

Growing your network is one of the best ways to prepare for the inevitable glaciers you'll face throughout your career.

BE A GENEROUS NETWORKER

When I was single, my good friend shared an unwritten rule for dating I'd never heard. He said, "You can't kiss her until you find out her middle name." Now, I don't know if this rule is applicable in today's dating scene—I've been happily married for a while now—but in a way, you can apply this tactic to your professional network.

No one likes the networker who tries to sell you something, or asks you for a favor, as soon as they find out your name. They could at least buy you a drink first. To be a Leader Assistant, learn how to be a *generous* networker. As you're connecting with people, in person or online, keep this question on the top of your mind: *"How can I truly help this person at this moment?"*

Helping could mean you listen to them rant about their day. It could mean you suggest a software tool that solves the exact problem they're wrestling with. You could introduce them to a friend in their industry or share their blog post with your LinkedIn network.

Notice how none of these examples involve you getting something out of them. In other words, help others, *but don't keep score.* If you help people without an expectation they will owe you something in return, you'll master the art of networking—and grow a high-quality, game-changing network.

NETWORKING AS AN INTROVERT

I can keep a conversation going for hours with Meg, my brothers, or my best friends, but throw me into a room full of strangers, and I'm spent after about eleven minutes. If you can relate, you're probably an introvert like me. Sure, I've developed my extroverted skills over the years, but I still love me some "me time."

Here are some tips on how to network as an introvert.

START SMALL

Don't go to an event with one hundred assistants and expect to meet every single one of them, remember their names, and strike up a quality conversation. Start with a smaller meetup, or if a large event is all you can find, focus on a small corner of the room. Commit to meet three or four new people, and be prepared to ask a few go-to questions. "What's your favorite part about being an assistant?" and "What's one thing you wish you could change about your role?" are a couple of my favorites.

KNOW YOUR LIMITS

Give yourself permission to leave the party after you meet your goal, but keep going if your social juices get flowing. Just know your limits and don't push yourself too far past them. A good way for an introvert to burn out is to overdo it with social interaction.

DON'T JUST NETWORK—CONNECT

Networking is about connecting with people at a meaningful level. If you're like me, you get bored with small talk pretty quickly. You'd rather talk about a big problem you're having, or share a heartwarming story about your kids. The good news is, when you focus on a few people, you have more time to take conversations to a deeper level than "How's the weather?"

No matter how extroverted or introverted you are, engaging in relationships with other assistants is an investment that all game-changing Leader Assistants make.

SIX WAYS TO GROW YOUR LINKEDIN NETWORK

When I was in between jobs, I looked where most look when faced with a career change: my LinkedIn network. I thought LinkedIn was the ugly duckling of social networks, so it'd been years since I'd logged on. I might've had a few dozen connections at the time. As I began to "manage my professional identity," I noticed people were actively engaged—posting, commenting, sending messages, recommending people for new jobs, and participating in like-minded groups. I was shocked to discover the gold mine that was LinkedIn, and I instantly regretted my lack of participation.

After spending a few years networking on all of the major online social platforms, LinkedIn consistently stood out as the best place to meet and interact with assistants. So I tried out a variety of methods to increase my LinkedIn connections and followers. Most failed, but I eventually discovered a few methods that worked, and I was able to grow my LinkedIn network from 2,800 to 16,700+ people in around ten months.

The following six tactics helped me achieve this growth, and I still use these today.

1. REACH OUT TO ASSISTANTS IN YOUR CITY

One of the most effective ways to grow your LinkedIn network is to reach out to assistants in your area and invite them to join you for happy hour, lunch, coffee, etc. LinkedIn makes this very easy for you to do. Visit **leaderassistantbook.com/bonus** for a link to my LinkedIn guide, where I share step-by-step instructions on how to perform an advanced search for assistants in your area.

2. CONNECT WITH ASSISTANTS AROUND THE WORLD

In today's world, it's easy to connect with assistants on the other side of the planet. There's no reason you can't build a professional relationship with an assistant just because they're not within driving distance.

Here's an example of what you could say when reaching out to assistants outside of your city:

> "Hi [First Name] - I've been an assistant for several years, but I've failed to grow my network. I'm hoping to change that and would love to connect and learn from you. Would you be up for connecting?"

3. THOUGHTFULLY ENGAGE IN ONLINE THREADS

Don't just "like" everything. Leave thoughtful comments on other posts you find interesting. Ask questions, and share with friends who would think the topic is interesting. Don't be a passive consumer; be an active user who contributes to the global assistant community.

When you do engage in online conversations, don't ask manipulative or passive-aggressive questions to start a debate. Also, don't talk down to people. You're not going to build trust and add value if you're always critiquing, judging, or looking to stir the pot.

4. WRITE ENGAGING POSTS ON LINKEDIN

Start your own conversations by posting statuses or articles on your LinkedIn profile. I usually post about topics I'm passionate about or experienced in. My most commented-on, "liked," and shared posts are ones in which I ask for input from the assistant community. I'll ask people to comment if they can relate. I'll often provide a short list of multiple-choice answers so they can engage with the post without having to type out a long answer. The more I limit the work needed to interact with a given post, the more people engage with it.

Whatever you decide to share, remember to add value to the broader community.

5. SWITCH YOUR "CONNECT" BUTTON TO THE "FOLLOW" BUTTON

If you get traffic to your profile because you're more active on LinkedIn or you have another website sending people to your LinkedIn profile, this tactic can work very well.

You can change the main "Connect" button on your profile to a "Follow" button. This gives people the opportunity to follow you with just one click when they're viewing your profile, instead of them having to hit "Connect," decide if they're going to "Add a Note" or not, then come up with something to say in that note.

To give you some context, today I have 13,900+ connections, but I have 18,300+ followers. My followers can still see and engage with my posts; I'm just not connected with them, and I don't follow them. As of now, there's a limit to how many connections you can have, but no limit to how many followers you can have. I can't promise you that making this switch will work as well for you as it has for me, but it's worth looking into.

6. IMPROVE YOUR PROFILE'S VISIBILITY

You can manipulate profile settings to help more people connect with you, and increase the odds that people will accept your requests when you reach out.

First, make sure your profile picture is visible to those who aren't connected to you. I personally hold off on sending or accepting connections if I can't see a profile picture. It communicates to me that you're either not real or not that engaged on the platform. Speaking of pictures, you'll want to showcase a professional profile picture (headshot) *and* a solid banner image (not the generic LinkedIn one).

Next, make your summary and bio visible to those who aren't connected with you. How are others going to be interested in networking with you if they don't know anything about you? Recruiters and executives looking to hire a Leader Assistant would like to read your bio and summary.

Lastly, edit your privacy settings to show your education and work history to those you're not connected with. The point of LinkedIn is to expand your professional network, so don't be shy.

Have fun, spice up your profile, and happy networking!

TWENTY-ONE

YOUR EXECUTIVE

———

My assistant sees, understands, and drives things in a way that I can't. She supports and guides me in a way that leads me to lead better.

—DON H., CEO (COLORADO SPRINGS, CO)

Once you have a strong support network of assistants who have your back and call you on your BS (BS = bull spit, if you're curious), you'll be empowered to engage in the next key relationship: your relationship with your executive.

To clarify, when I say "engage," I don't mean you storm into your executive's office to shout orders and blame them for your high blood pressure (even if it's true). I also don't mean you avoid eye contact or walk into your one-on-one with your head down. Instead, confidently have conversations with your executive that lead to game-changing results for you both.

Your relationship with your executive should be professional, strategic, and mutually supportive. Your goal is to help them succeed, and their goal is to help you succeed. The following lessons I've learned over the years will help you build a winning partnership as you engage in your relationship with your executive.

DON'T BE A HERO

You save the day for your executive all the time. You bend over backwards behind the scenes to help them succeed. One could argue you're a hero to your executive, and in many ways you are.

But should you see yourself primarily as the hero in your executive's story?

Donald Miller is an author and CEO of a marketing business called StoryBrand. His company uses an age-old framework to help businesses not see themselves as the hero coming to save the day for their customers. Instead, he urges businesses to invite their customers into a story where the customer is always the hero.

Miller likes to use Star Wars as an example. Luke Skywalker is the hero who saves the day by destroying the Death Star. Yoda is one of a few key guides who help Luke along his hero's journey. In the StoryBrand framework, a business is Yoda—the guide to help the hero customer, Luke, conquer the glaciers along their journey.

I love this framework because it takes the customer's focus off of how awesome a business is. Instead, it shifts the customer's attention to how that business can help the customer win the battle they're fighting. A business should strive to be Yoda, not Luke.

The same goes for you, if you want to be a game-changing Leader

Assistant. You are the guide in your executive's journey. After all, if they succeed in conquering the evil Empire, you win too. Let's look at your resume as an example of how this framework plays out practically. If you see yourself as the hero, your resume might lead with "I've been an assistant for twenty-three years." If you see yourself as the guide, however, your resume might lead with "I help you save time. Period." Notice the difference?

Don't get me wrong, I'm all about you being confident and proud of your experience and what you've accomplished throughout your career. You can even wear a red cape if you'd like. But your executive doesn't care about your credentials unless those credentials show what you can do for them.

Think of yourself as Yoda—the guide who helps the hero (your executive and company) win. You're not the hero.

COMMUNICATING WITH YOUR EXECUTIVE

As I type this, my boys are playing with LEGO in the next room. At the moment, they're playing very well together, and it's one of the sweetest sounds I've ever heard.

(As soon as I was done typing the above sentence, Weston came in with his fidget spinner UFO and tiny alien and walked it all over my desk. It was very sweet until I realized his hand—the one that just took a tour of my mouse and keyboard—was covered in snot. Ah, the joys of parenting.)

If I'm lucky, my boys will get through this play session without incident. But these precious moments of play often halt abruptly with a "Dad, Silas won't let me have the blue LEGO!" or "Dad, Weston took my red LEGO!" In these moments of communication breakdown, I tend to ask the following question: "Did you nicely ask your brother for what you want?" Nine times out of ten they answer, "Well, no."

In other words, my boys often fail to communicate. The more I coach assistants through their own communication issues, the more I'm convinced that—just as with my LEGO-loving boys—open dialogue is the key to a productive working relationship.

The other day I was on a coaching call with an assistant who said she wanted to be a leader and take more initiative with her executive but didn't know where to start. I asked her how often she and her executive meet together. She said they rarely, if ever, get time to meet.

Another assistant told me she meets regularly with her executive but has a similar problem: she doesn't know how to level up and make more impact with her executive. Her issue isn't a lack of face-to-face meetings, but a lack of intentional structure and conversations in those meetings.

QUESTIONS AREN'T A SIGN OF WEAKNESS

How can you improve communication with your executive? You can start by regularly asking your executive questions to understand the "why" behind what they do, and to ensure you're on the same page. Ask a lot of clarifying questions if you want to anticipate and read your executive's mind to improve productivity and efficiency.

Questions aren't a sign of weakness, they're a sign of leadership. Think about a few of the best conversations you've ever had.

Or the most interesting podcast interviews you've listened to. Or the best counseling or therapy session you were a part of. What was the common thread in all of these? They were full of good questions.

If you're just starting off with a new executive, ask more questions than you might be comfortable with. If you've been with the same executive for several years, you won't need to ask as many questions, but never stop asking. You're not perfect, and you're not your executive, so don't be afraid to ask.

As I mentioned earlier in the book, I was the de facto accountant for our startup during its first year of existence. I supervised a large budget in my previous role at a nonprofit, but I'd never worked at a for-profit before. I knew nothing about how our CEO wanted the numbers crunched, so I annoyed him with countless clarifying questions.

In the long run, my questioning made things easier on our eventual accounting manager and CFO because I had things at least partially set up the way our CEO wanted it from the beginning. In fact, we were audited by the IRS for that year I managed the books, and we passed with flying colors. I'm glad I asked lots of questions.

Does your executive encourage your questioning or express frustration when you speak up? If it's uncomfortable for you to speak openly and ask questions of your executive, be honest with yourself about why. Is it because you're intimidated by your executive? If so, why? Did something happen between you two? Did you have a previous executive who would verbally abuse you if you dared ask a question? Are you silent because you simply don't know what to ask?

QUESTIONS TO ASK YOUR EXECUTIVE

Let's go over some specific questions you can ask your executive to help you be proactive and anticipate their needs. You probably don't want to ask all of these in one sitting, so spread them out across a few one-on-one meetings. Also, arrive prepared with a suggested answer to each question in case your executive is stumped. Finally, be sure to take notes, make an action plan, then revisit that plan in a few weeks.

What's one thing I could do to make your job less stressful this week?

Your job is to make your executive's job easier, so cut to the chase, ask this question, and be ready to propose an answer. It could be as simple as grabbing lunch for them when they don't have time to grab it themselves, or as complicated as formatting a fifty-nine-page PowerPoint presentation for the upcoming board meeting. Don't ask if you're not willing to get your hands dirty.

In what ways do I frustrate you? How would you recommend I change?

This question gets the most cringes when I share it during my training or speaking engagements. It's certainly a humbling question to ask, and puts you in a vulnerable position, but if your executive is frustrated about something you are or aren't doing—you want to know.

In your next one-on-one, frame this question casually. You could say, "I've been working on my professional development in general, but one of the things I'm curious about is if there's something about the way I work that frustrates you. If so, I'd like to consider ways I can improve and be more helpful to you."

When I asked one of my executives this question, he said he wished I didn't ping him about minor details throughout the day. Instead, he suggested we go over small details once or twice a week to limit distractions. It was hard to hear at the time, but it was an invaluable tip. I've now used this tactic for years, and every executive loves it.

What's my greatest strength? Do you believe this strength is being utilized? If not, what changes could we make to get more out of me in this area?

You might be really good at writing communications to the entire company, but does your executive give you the opportunity to do so? Or are they asking you to run pointless errands all the time? Ask them this question so you can begin to work more from your strengths. Again, you'll want to be ready to answer these questions to show you're self-aware and ready for action.

Is there a task or project you're working on that I could take care of?

Don't let your executive micromanage or work on tasks that aren't in their job description. You might already have a list of tasks you can take off their plate, so have this list with you.

Could we rearrange our calendars to make things easier, more enjoyable, and more productive for you?

The answer to this question should always be "Yes." Be aware of the meetings your executive should or should not be attending. Make it a priority to sit down with them and do an audit of their calendar like I discuss in chapter 10.

How can I help you prioritize your to-do list?

Many executives know what they need to do, but they get overwhelmed and don't know where to begin. You can help them break their to-do list into bite-sized tasks. You can then work with them to prioritize the list so they don't miss anything important.

LEARN TO LEAD

I realize asking these questions can be intimidating. It takes courage and maturity to be vulnerable, especially if your executive is resistant. But I've never regretted asking. I always take something away that helps me lead better. In fact, these questions often spark some of the best strategic business conversations we've had—you know, the types of conversations entrepreneurs and MBA students would pay a lot of money to be a part of.

SAY NO TO YOUR EXECUTIVE

I discussed saying no in chapter 9, but I want to talk about this tactic specifically as it relates to your relationship with your executive.

As a Leader Assistant, be willing to say no to your executive.

There are times when your executive will ask you to do something, but you know it will take your focus off of higher-priority tasks. Instead of just adding it to your to-do list, consider pushing back. Ask your executive if that task can be offloaded to another team member or disregarded completely. When an executive says they want something done, they usually mean it. But I've found that if you remind them of the big picture, they'll rethink whether a task is necessary.

When my previous executive was fired, he and I sat down and debriefed what happened. We talked about several times I'd told him no or strongly advised him against a decision, yet he didn't listen. He regretfully admitted he should've listened to me more. I often wonder: If I would've been more firm, would things have turned out differently for him? I don't blame myself for his failures, but I did learn that sometimes it's OK to be more assertive when saying no to an executive.

WORKING WITH A MICROMANAGER

I have a confession to make: I'm a control freak. I like things done the right way. Of course, when I say "the right way," I mean "my way." If someone does something well—but not exactly the way I like it done—I'll do everything in my power to correct it. I'm sure Meg would be happy to tell you more about my condition.

I'm not proud to be an experienced and gifted micromanager. But there are times when it seems micromanaging is the only way to get anything done.

At one of our offsite strategic leadership meetings, I ordered lunch for the entire group. There was a restaurant on the other end of the block, so I figured it would be a safe option for getting food for sixteen people in a timely manner. I debated picking up the order myself, but I didn't want to miss any of the discussion. I also thought to myself, "Jeremy, you don't have to do everything. Just have them deliver it." You can probably guess where this story is headed.

The delivery driver picked up our order and someone else's at the same time. Instead of looking to see how close we were, he decided to deliver our order second. As it turned out, the order he chose to deliver first was twenty minutes away.

Our food failed to arrive on time, so I called the restaurant to ask where it was. They said the driver was on his way, so all I could do was pace back and forth as a room full of hungry team members waited for me. I kept thinking, "I should've picked up the food myself. If I would've micromanaged, the team would've gotten their lunch on time." When lunch finally did arrive, it was an hour late.

As an assistant, you experience moments like this all the time. But do you know who else deals with inefficient and incompetent people on a regular basis? Your executive. So the next time your executive breathes down your neck about something, try putting yourself in their shoes.

Maybe they've been at the mercy of a team that doesn't finish the graphics in time for their presentation. Or they've missed a deadline because the communications team created a video that totally missed the vision they were trying to convey. In other words, your executive knows what it's like to think, "I should've taken care of it myself." They know how difficult it is to trust others.

Have you thought about what motivates your executive to micromanage?

The best way to encourage your executive to be less controlling and more trusting is to recognize—and help them see—*why* they micromanage. From there, you can lead your executive out of their controlling ways.

Here are three common motivations behind our tendency to

micromanage. Make a note of which ones are more likely to cause your executive to be controlling. These motivations will also give you language to use when bringing this topic up with your executive.

1. CONTROL

Your executive might micromanage because they feel like they're losing control of some aspect of their life. It could be unrelated to you. Maybe it's a board member, a department lead, or even a rebellious teenager at home. Are they grasping for what they can control out of desperation? Be aware of the entire context of the situation, especially if your executive is a seasonal micromanager.

2. COMPLETING A TASK

Your executive works on initiatives or projects that take months, maybe even years, to complete. Because there's so much time between completing these projects, they can feel unproductive for months. To combat this lack of momentum, they might want to build a quick slide deck, schedule a meeting, or see another quick task to completion. Several times throughout the process of writing this book, I've found myself taking a break to reply to an email or post a quick thought on social media—you know, things I can check off a list in a few minutes to feel accomplished.

This is why many executives struggle to delegate simple tasks, and even when they do, they micromanage. They don't want to miss the thrill of seeing something get done. They want to feel productive. Is this your executive's motivation for micromanaging? If so, help your executive break their long-term projects into parts they can measure on a short-term basis. In other words, if they see progress along the way, perhaps they won't feel so unproductive.

3. EXCELLENCE

There are times when I want things to be done with excellence, and I do my best to help others succeed. In these situations, my goal is to equip and empower. However, if I don't trust the other person to do a good job, I hurt the situation, not help it. My micromanaging takes away any space for that person to figure it out on their own. In other words, I'm not setting them up to succeed. I'm not empowering them toward excellence. I'm not delegating well. I'm simply doing everything for them while they watch.

Is excellence your executive's motivation? Think about the last time they micromanaged you. Was it necessary for them to be so involved? Or was it simply a personal preference? Was their motivation truly excellence and productivity, or did they just want to maintain control? Can you gently show them your track record of excellence to ease their fears?

DELEGATE RESULTS

Never tell people how to do things. Tell them what to do and they will surprise you with their ingenuity.

—FORMER ARMY GEN. GEORGE PATTON

Now that you have an idea of what's behind your executive's desire to micromanage, you can help them learn to delegate *results*—not just tasks. In short, your executive should explain the "why" and let you figure out the "what" and "how." If you need help along the way, your executive can make themselves available.[3]

Here's an Example of Delegating a Task

Your executive asks you to schedule a meeting with all eleven board members, over a nice dinner, at an off-site location, before the end of the year. The next day, your executive texts each board member to ask what day works for the meeting. Then they call a couple of restaurants to reserve a room.

A couple of days later, your executive calls you to tell you a few date options and mentions they found a great restaurant. You let them know you already booked a different restaurant. They tell you to call so-and-so to get a third option just in case.

Later that day, your executive texts the board again to ask where they'd like to have the meeting. After gathering a few responses, they ask you to visit each restaurant to get a feel for what the best option would be.

The next day, your executive decides to visit a couple of the restaurants, then books a room at one of them. When they call you later, you inform them you've already visited all three and booked a room at one of the other options.

This whole time you're thinking to yourself, "Great. I just wasted my time on all this while you did the work. And you wasted your time on it even though you have bigger fish to fry!"

---

3   *I first heard about the concept of delegating results versus tasks from Bryan Miles, co-founder and former CEO of BELAY Solutions, the largest virtual assistant firm in the US.*

Here's an Example of Delegating Results

Your executive asks you to schedule a meeting with all eleven board members, over a nice dinner, at an off-site location, before the end of the year. Your executive tells you to let them know if you have any questions or run into any issues along the way. They go back to working on the agenda for the meeting—and other key projects—as they await your updates. You book the restaurant, and all is well.

TRUST AND LEAD

Notice the difference? Your executive can stop micromanaging and start leading well by delegating results—no matter what their motivations are. Your job is to help them overcome the poor leadership practice of micromanaging and learn to delegate results.

Lead your executive by giving them specific examples of times they've delegated tasks when they could've delegated results. Walk them through your examples and show them how delegating results would've looked. Ask them if they'd be willing to try it differently for the next project.

WORKING WITH A RESISTANT EXECUTIVE

If your executive is resistant to you engaging them, consider the following alternative ways to approach them.

First, your executive might not like being put on the spot. Instead of asking questions, you could present proposals and suggestions. For example, don't ask, "How can I help you prioritize your to-do list?" Instead, say, "Here is your prioritized to-do list for the week. Did I miss anything?" Sometimes you don't need to ask your executive how to help; instead, show them how *you've already helped.*

Another way to work with a resistant executive is to have an open conversation with them. Of course, how you frame the conversation is critical. Make the conversation about helping them, not about how you wish they weren't so difficult. Let them know you want to take on more responsibility so they have more capacity to succeed. If you've attempted this conversation with no luck, consider asking an HR representative to attend the meeting as a mediator.

Initiating a meeting like this can lead to a few worst-case scenarios. Your executive could be a defensive jerk, verbally abuse you, or even fire you for being nosy. As tough as these scenarios would be, the quicker you can move on from a toxic environment, the better. If you've tried different ways to engage in your relationship with your executive, but they won't respond, it's time to move on. I know it's easier said than done, but confident, game-changing Leader Assistants don't put up with abusive relationships.

Before you defend your executive and claim they aren't abusive, remember that avoidance is a form of abuse. Maybe your executive isn't actively abusive or disrespectful, but they *are* lazy and lack leadership skills. Your life is too short and your career is too important to work for an executive who fails to challenge you, draw the best out of you, and support you.

SUPPORTING MULTIPLE EXECUTIVES

If you have more than one executive, you can apply the above tactics and questions to each executive. The key is to know their unique communication styles (as discussed in chapter 18) and adapt accordingly. If you have a few executives and one of them is difficult, but the others are great, talk to the difficult one. Give them examples of systems and methods you and the other executives have found to be helpful. Show them data to quantify the success you've had with the other executives.

Do you want to cultivate an unstoppable strategic partnership? Engage in thoughtful conversations, learn to say no, ask questions, and lead your executive out of their micromanaging ways.

TWENTY-TWO

YOUR COWORKERS

———

Great relationships are what make an assistant a leader. I'm not saying strive to be popular—far from it. Leadership isn't a popularity contest. So much of what we do is built on relationships—with our co-workers, our clients, our executives, other assistants, even vendors. If you can forge and maintain good relationships with people, especially over the lifespan of a career, you don't label yourself as a leader—others do.

—ANGELIC V., FOUNDER AND CEO (ST. LOUIS, MO)

There was a time when all of my best friends were coworkers. I thought nothing of it until one day I found out one of them was about to get fired. I had to hold on to this confidential information for days before it happened.

Knowing a friend is about to lose their job is not a fun burden to carry.

Around that same time, some of my coworkers befriended me just to get closer to my executive (their boss). The combination of dehumanizing interactions and watching my friends get fired exhausted me emotionally and contributed to my disengagement at work. For my final few years in that role, I was cordial but reserved and cautious with my relationships at work. I intentionally chose *not* to be best friends with coworkers.

TO BEFRIEND, OR NOT TO BEFRIEND?

Befriending coworkers *seems* like a great idea. If you're able to keep confidential information to yourself, and not expose it in conversations at the bar, there's nothing wrong with it. Why not enjoy the people you work with?

But it's very difficult to become *best* friends with a coworker and keep the relationship professional.

I'm still not sure whether I think it's best to keep your business and social life completely separate. Some days I think being friends with coworkers is a terrible idea. Other days I think being friends with each and every one of your coworkers is the only way to go. Either way, it's critical to have close friends *outside* of work—friends you can be real with, have fun with, or grab a drink with while you forget about your job. These close friends can be family members, old college buddies, or assistants from other companies.

Be friendly with coworkers, but find your best friends outside of the office.

RELATING TO COWORKERS

How should we relate to coworkers if not as best friends? Be generous and caring. Strike up conversations in the break room. Encourage someone who's feeling down. Ask them how their dogs or kids are doing. But keep things professional. Don't start gossiping about your executive or spreading information that belongs in the boardroom. Instead, ask your coworkers what they like about working there so you can get a feel for how the company is doing. Ask them what they would change about the office. Ask for their opinion on what the company is doing poorly. Ask them if there's anything you can do to help.

Leader Assistants are in tune with their company's culture by listening to and connecting with coworkers from all departments and levels.

LEADERS ARE NOT ELITIST

Have you ever been frustrated with other assistants because they seem perfectly content to just do what they're told, and they lack a desire to shape culture, grow their influence, or have a bigger impact? Do you get frustrated with assistants who are struggling to fulfill their duties?

Instead of looking down at assistants who seem to lack the skills of or desire for leadership, what if you choose to invest in and encourage them? What if, with open arms, you invite them to embrace and own their role?

Equip, empower, and grow together with other assistants—no matter their experience. Instead of a sense of elitism, cultivate a culture of growth and humility in the global assistant community.

PUSHING CARTS AT WALMART (AND COMPANY CULTURE)

Speaking of culture, I learned a valuable lesson about company culture when I was a teenager pushing carts at Walmart. I worked in the pet department, stocking cat litter and dog food, and selling goldfish in plastic bags to customers I knew would be back the following week in search of a replacement "Goldie."

During a particularly hot and humid summer, one assistant manager made a habit of instructing me to go out to the parking lot in the heat to retrieve all the shopping carts. This kind of request wasn't out of the ordinary, but there was a period that summer when it happened several nights in a row.

I was normally happy to help out. After all, it mixed up my evenings a bit and kept things interesting. However, Walmart's dress code didn't allow employees to wear shorts on the sales floor. My work uniform included heavy khaki jeans, which aren't the most comfortable attire for pushing heavy carts around a steaming asphalt parking lot.

After a few nights of this, I asked the assistant manager if I could wear shorts to work—just in case I was asked to push carts again. He firmly replied, "No, you need to stick to the dress code." I was frustrated by his "by-the-book" management style, so I mentioned it to my direct supervisor the next day. To keep this book safe for work, I'll just say my supervisor was not happy.

The next night, I went to work with my pants on (as most do) and got a call from the "no shorts for you!" assistant manager. I assumed I was being beckoned to the pavement again. Instead, he apologized for asking me to push carts in the extreme heat without the proper attire. He told me if the temperature was hotter than ninety degrees, I could wear shorts to work—just in case they needed me outside. At the time, I was just happy to wear shorts for my next shift. I didn't realize the long-term impact that day would have on me.

I later discovered my supervisor called the store manager, who then told the assistant manager to apologize to me for his bad judgment. When my dad found out about this, he said, "Son, be grateful for working with that team. It's extremely rare for someone above your paygrade to apologize and admit their wrongdoing."

At a young age, I was exposed to a simple yet powerful tool for building a healthy company culture: an apology. It's not easy to admit we're wrong. It's not the cool thing to do, either, especially in professional settings. Many of us are afraid we'll be exposed as frauds. We hide behind the one thing we think we have going for us: being right all the time. But deep down, we know we're wrong much of the time.

A CULTURE OF ACCOUNTABILITY

Since that day at Walmart, I've been blessed to work in corporate cultures that encourage the practice of admitting mistakes.

I know this isn't the norm and that apologizing is seen as weakness in many circles, but Leader Assistants contribute to building a healthy culture of accountability in the workplace. They don't get defensive and point their finger at others. They own up to their mistakes. Sometimes they even take responsibility for something that wasn't completely their fault. A Leader Assistant follows the words of John Maxwell: "Leadership is taking responsibility while others are making excuses."

You can also build a culture of accountability by asking others to apologize. If you have your executive's ear, let them know when they need to admit a mistake. Encourage other team members to own their screw-ups as well. For example, if someone else was wrong or did something inappropriate, ask them to apologize to those affected. If it was a public offense, ask them to make it right in public. If it was a private offense, make sure they address it privately. When you have the opportunity to be a champion for accountability, integrity, and transparency, seize it. You can choose to confidently lead or let opportunities to build a healthy culture pass by.

One of my coworkers made a jab at one of our new interns on Slack, our instant messaging tool. It was pretty harsh, but they had been friends long before working together, so no offense was taken. However, the jab was on the entire company's group channel—not an appropriate place for a friendly insult. And without going into details, it did not read like a friendly jab to most of us.

I suggested the offender's supervisor ask the offender to apologize on the group channel. I told the leadership team I thought it would set a good precedent for the culture of our company. They all agreed, and the offender apologized. It was a key moment in the evolution of our company's culture, and to this day, the offending team member is a valuable contributor to our organization.

Another example of apologizing came from the top of our corporate ladder. Our CEO once made a comment that came across as if he was saying those who assemble furniture for our office are doing less important work than the work of our software developers. A few team members who put together desks took offense to his comment. He could've easily gotten defensive and told the offended parties to get over it. Instead, he genuinely owned his mistake and apologized to the entire company.

How about you? Did you screw up an itinerary? Did you forget to follow up with someone? Did you quote a stat that was incorrect? Did you say something inappropriate? Odds are if you're like me and every other human being on the planet, you've made a mistake or two in your life, and probably in the last couple of days. It's time to own your errors and move on. Is there someone you need to apologize to? Find this person ASAP and admit you were wrong. The longer you wait, the more difficult—and less meaningful—your apology will be.

Now, before you go around saying, "I'm sorry," for every little thing that happens, remember you can rephrase some of your apologies. For example, instead of saying, "I'm sorry I'm late," you can say, "Thank you for waiting for me." That said, *don't stop apologizing completely*. There are times when a remorseful "I'm sorry I said what I said" is necessary.

DONUTS AND DIGNITY

I love donuts, but I *really* love Eddie's Southtown Donuts in St. Louis. We used to live down the street and would walk or ride our bikes there every weekend. There's even a cold-pressed juice spot next door for a healthy drink to wash down our not-so-healthy treat.

But what makes Eddie's so great is we get to talk to Eddie himself when we visit. He treats us with respect. We talk about football, business, and more. He calls us the "blueberry family" because I always get his blueberry-glazed donut—it's the best one I've ever had—and we walk out with a couple of extra donuts Eddie slipped in our bag without us noticing.

There's something special about walking into Eddie's. It's like we take a step back in time, before the world of shallow social media "likes" and robot cashiers. It reminds me of our humanity, and it's one of the few moments when my boys get a glimpse of a simpler time.

We no longer live down the street, so we don't visit Eddie's *quite* as often as we used to. But Eddie still treats us like regulars. We still walk in to see a familiar face, and we still walk out with a couple of extra donuts.

Seeing how Eddie runs his donut shop has taught me a lot about respect and dignity, and it can be applied at work too. You might only interact with the janitor once a month, or the parking-lot attendant for a few seconds a day, but that's no reason to treat them as any less of a human. Don't be a stranger to the people you interact with.

Leader Assistants treat *everyone* with dignity.

LEADER ASSISTANTS ARE TEAM PLAYERS

The last thing I'll say about your relationships with coworkers is this: always be willing to help. I don't care if it's the janitorial, marketing, sales, or product team. If you see a piece of trash on the floor, pick it up. If you notice an issue with the product, create a ticket. If you see an opportunity for brand exposure, point it out. If you meet someone at an event who could use your services, set up a demo with the sales team.

Engage in relationships at work by being a team player.

EXERCISE SELF-CARE

Leader Assistants know when to slow down and exercise self-care.

I feel a sense of significance when I play even a small role in someone else's success. Because of this, I'm always on the lookout for opportunities to help others. Helpfulness is a great quality to embody, and it has served me well in my career as an assistant.

However, my healthy desire to help others often becomes an unhealthy excuse to prioritize work over my family and my health.

I've worked far too many seventy-hour weeks under the guise of being extra helpful. When I overwork, I burn out because I fail to invest in my mental, spiritual, physical, social, and emotional health. And when I burn out, I'm unable to help anyone.

Exercising self-care is the key to long-term sustainability. You can master the first three pillars, but if you don't take care of yourself, you'll eventually burn out. And burnout poisons us, making us weak and unbalanced. Of course, you can't have perfect balance in every area of your life. But you can have the self-awareness to know when one or more areas need to be realigned.

Let's learn to attack burnout—the enemy of well-being—by exploring how burnout can creep up on us, how to recognize stressors that make us vulnerable to burnout, how to spot the signs of burnout, and the five antidotes to burnout.

TWENTY-THREE

BURNOUT CREEP

——

Do something, but don't do everything.

—ANONYMOUS

As I dug a hole in my executive's backyard for his soon-to-be-dead dog—the same dog who had a thing for my leg as a puppy more than a decade prior—I had mixed feelings. On one hand, I was glad to help my executive and longtime friend while he was out of town. His in-laws were dog-sitting but weren't physically capable of burying the poor dog if it were to pass on their watch.

On the other hand, I had a sense something wasn't right about the whole scenario. Yes, I was the executive assistant *and* personal assistant, but was I being taken advantage of in this moment? If not, were there other times I'd been asked to do tasks that crossed the line? Was I too willing to serve?

Unfortunately, I didn't stop long enough to answer my questions that day. Instead, I pushed them aside and kept sticking my executive's shovel into the dry dirt.

Another dog and a few years later, I was in the passenger seat of that same executive's truck. We were on our way to pick up his kids from school. He noticed something was bothering me and asked if I was OK. "Not really," I said as I explained that I was exhausted and burned out. He said he wondered why I'd been "such an asshole of late." It sounds harsh, but he was right. We'd been running at an unsustainable pace for a while, and I hadn't been myself because of it. I didn't have anything left in the tank. Something needed to change quickly or I was going to continue to be an unpleasant person.

He suggested I work remotely from my hometown of Kansas City that next month—which happened to be during the Royals' playoff run. This gave me freedom to be with family and friends and attend Royals baseball games—one of my favorite things to do. I attended every game in KC that October. I even had the opportunity to be at Games 4 and 5 of the World Series in NYC to see the Royals win it all—a lifelong dream come true. To this day, I'm grateful my executive gave me time and space to slow down and separate myself from harmful work rhythms. I'm not sure I would've lasted much longer without quitting (or something worse) if not for that month of working remotely.

A few months later, that same executive made mistakes that cost him his job—and burnout was a major contributing factor.

I wish I could say that he and I are the only people I've seen damaged by burnout. Unfortunately, I know several people with destroyed relationships, careers, families, physical and emotional health, and more—all due to burnout. When you burn out, you don't think straight or see clearly. Your body shuts down. You get desperate. You say and do things you'll regret.

And unfortunately, burnout doesn't just jump out and announce itself.

BURNOUT CREEP

Burnout is tricky because it creeps up when you least expect it. If I had seen my, or my previous executive's, burnout coming— and understood its consequences—I would've tried to prevent it. Instead, it took him getting fired and me getting stuck in the middle of my career glacier for me to realize how unhealthy I was.

I worked long hours because I was addicted to the rush of accomplishing tasks and helping others. I was *too* willing to serve, even when I was being taken advantage of. I rarely took a day off, and when I did, I saw it as an opportunity to work more.

Being busy was my excuse to be lazy when it came to caring for myself and my family. Work was my life: a slow-cooker recipe for burnout.

Work is no longer my life, but I still love to work, so I'll always have to fight burnout creep. For example, yesterday I planned to spend a few hours writing. As I sat down at my laptop, I realized I was exhausted. But instead of pushing through my exhaustion like I do so often, I closed my laptop and spent the rest of the day with my family. It was a small but powerful attack on burnout. I had an amazing time connecting with Meg and the boys, and the next day I was reenergized.

LIMITING THE EFFECTS OF BURNOUT

This is where I'm supposed to reveal a list of tricks to help you eliminate any chance of burnout. Well, I hate to break it to you, but if you're trying to be a leader, there's nothing you can do to completely avoid it. If you haven't already, you *will* burn out at some point in your life. In fact, burnout is the most common glacier you'll face.

But don't lose heart—exercising self-care will help you limit the effects of burnout.

Your desire to do more and be more is not inherently bad. However, far too often a desire to produce ends up not producing anything but exhaustion, lack of clarity, and ultimately burnout. It's time to hit the reset button before you crash and burn.

We're going to explore the following elements of self-care to wrap up our journey:

- Recognizing the stressors that can drive you to burnout
- Spotting the signs of burnout taking root in your life
- Resisting burnout with five practical antidotes

Let's exercise self-care together.

TWENTY-FOUR

BURNOUT STRESSORS AND SIGNS

———

Something doesn't feel right, but you're too busy to figure out what it is. You're stressed and exhausted, but everyone else is too, so you keep grinding. You tell yourself people don't care how healthy you are; they just want you to produce. The next thing you know, you don't have anything left in the tank.

If you're lucky, you notice your burnout before you end up in the hospital with stress-induced illness, or end up doing something you can't take back—like cheat on your partner, steal money from your employer, or fall into substance abuse.

Do you see how your failure to take care of yourself limits your capacity for excellent work? If you're suffering from burnout or are heading in that direction, how can you make drastic changes before it's too late?

THE STRESSORS

The first element of self-care is recognizing the following five stressors that leave you prone to burnout.

STRESSOR #1: A MISMATCH
You're stressed when...

You're mismatched with your executive. There are many possible types of mismatches, but here are a few of them:

- **The Underqualified Mismatch:** Growth in your organization resulted in a more demanding, fast-paced environment, and you're struggling to keep up with new expectations from your executive. You're unsure whether the answer is a new executive or a new organization, but you're longing for a taste of success.
- **The Overqualified Mismatch:** You've outgrown your role and aren't challenged by your executive, so you're bored.
- **The Passion Mismatch:** Your job description looks nothing like what you were hired for. You're fully capable of fulfilling the role, but it's uninteresting and draining the life out of you. This shift in your role doesn't drive you to overwork, but it kills your passion for work, causing you undue stress.
- **The Values Mismatch:** You and your executive don't share the same values. You're a high achiever, but your executive is not. You value integrity, but your executive cares more about the bottom line. Value differences cause tension in your relationship.

What now?

If you're in an underqualified, overqualified, or values mismatch, talk to a career coach or someone outside of your organization you're close to. Admit you're mismatched with your executive, and it's causing you stress. Investigate what changes can be made to your role, or consider finding a new job.

If you're in a passion mismatch, sort through your current projects and tasks on a simple spreadsheet or piece of paper. Write down what you want and love to do on one side. On the other side, list the projects and tasks you're currently doing but loathe. Work through the list with your executive to determine if significant changes can be made. Revisit the five-step process in chapter 8 to work through this.

The emptiness, dissonance, or demands from a mismatch at work can easily drive you to burn out, so don't make light of it.

STRESSOR #2: MISSION DRIFT
You're stressed when...

Your organization moves away from its original mission. Sometimes this is an intentional change in direction. Other times, as organizations grow, they lose sight of why they were formed in the first place.

What now?

If the drift was unintentional, is your executive aware of it? Can you help them lead the charge to get the organization back on track? Dig in to determine whether there's any hope of reclaiming the original mission. If the drift was intentional, seriously consider the new mission to see if you can align with it. If you're not on board with it, it might be time to move on to an organization with a mission you believe in.

STRESSOR #3: NEW LIFE STAGE
You're stressed when...

You enter a new stage of life—you get older, have kids, get married, buy a home, develop health issues, etc. The changes at home add a new layer of emotional and physical stress.

What now?

See a counselor. Take a personal day. Restructure your calendar so you have more space to recover emotionally and physically.

STRESSOR #4: LACK OF TRUST
You're stressed when...

You don't trust your executive, the board of directors, human resources, or another coworker. If you don't trust your team members, you'll take on more work than needed. Not to mention, each interaction with a team member you distrust will be stressful.

What now?

Work through your lack of trust with that team member, perhaps even with a coach or an HR representative present. Get to the root of why you don't trust them, and work to rebuild the relationship. You're more prone to stress-induced burnout when trust is broken.

STRESSOR #5: THE "GRASS IS GREENER" SYNDROME
You're stressed when...

You've convinced yourself the grass is greener on the other side.

You think, "If only I worked at that other company," or "If only so and so wasn't on our team."

What now?

The truth is, most of the time it's not greener on the other side, so try to get to the root of why you think it is. Maybe another stressor listed here is the real reason for your discontent. If you know for a fact the grass is greener on the other side, why haven't you already hopped the fence?

KNOW YOUR STRESSORS

Which of the five stressors are more likely to drive you to burnout? Becoming aware of what might drive you to burnout is critical to exercising self-care.

THE SIGNS

The second element of self-care is to spot burnout taking root in your life. If you see the signs early, you can make powerful changes before those roots take hold. Keep an eye out for the following five signs of burnout.

SIGN #1: YOU'RE TIRED OR SICK ALL THE TIME

Do you find you're taking more sick days than others in the office? I'm not referring to chronic or other serious illnesses that are challenging to deal with. I'm talking about things like colds, flus, sinus infections, and other "standard illnesses." If those around you make comments about how you're sick all the time (this happened to me over and over), don't dismiss them. Your frequent illnesses could be a direct result of you working too much and pushing yourself too hard. Or maybe you get sick because you don't sleep enough.

How many cups of coffee do you need to stay alert throughout the day? Are you tired even after your day off? How much sleep do you get each night? If you're exhausted all the time, it can be due to many factors, but if you're not getting at least seven hours of sleep every night, your body will fight back. Go to bed early. Try other things to combat your sleepiness, too: eat healthy and don't eat after 8 p.m., exercise regularly, and remove all screens from your bedroom, including your phone.

SIGN #2: YOU'RE EASILY IRRITATED

A few years ago this was me. I was overworked and exhausted and, unfortunately, very irritable. If you don't believe me, you can ask Meg. There are more than a few verses in the Bible that talk about being "slow to anger." Unfortunately, they did not describe me at the time. If other people are frightened or on edge around you, consider it a warning: you might be in the midst of burnout.

SIGN #3: YOU DREAD GOING TO WORK

Does your blood pressure rise at the thought of heading into the office? Does your stomach sink when you park your car at work? This dread could be a sign that you've lost your passion and should find a new job. But maybe you don't need a new job; maybe you're just burned out. It might be that you still love your work and your company, but that you've been sprinting too long. That kind of pace is not sustainable. You need a break.

SIGN #4: YOU STOP CARING ABOUT PEOPLE

Have you caught yourself wishing ill will toward others? Are you uncharacteristically numb to the well-being of people you come in contact with? If you stop caring about people, you might not have a cold, dark heart—you might just be burned out. If you've never cared about people, that's a different issue.

SIGN #5: YOU CAN'T MAKE DECISIONS

This sign can be subtle, but if you struggle to make simple decisions, you could be burned out. I'm typically a quick decision-maker, so when I have a hard time deciding what shirt to wear or what meal to order at a restaurant, I know something isn't right. If you catch yourself struggling to make simple decisions, you can't trust yourself to make complex decisions. In the next chapter, I'll talk about reducing decision fatigue as an antidote to burnout.

DON'T IGNORE THE STRESSORS AND SIGNS

If you're experiencing any of these stressors and signs, don't ignore them. You're likely burning out. Let someone you trust know you're struggling. It's better for your partner, executive, or coworkers to find out now, versus finding out when you've become so burned out you get fired or quit.

TWENTY-FIVE

FIVE ANTIDOTES
TO BURNOUT

———

*A Leader Assistant has drive, confidence, adaptability, honesty,
integrity, and grit. Even on the hard days.*

—MEGAN E., EXECUTIVE ASSISTANT (AUSTIN, TX)

When you experience the stressors and begin to see the signs
of burnout, establish new habits and healthier rhythms as soon
as possible. The following habits or "antidotes" to burnout are
crucial not just for recovery, but also for shielding your career
against the stress of future glaciers. Whether you currently feel
energized or run-down, set your trajectory in the right direction with these five practical antidotes that will help you resist
burnout.

ANTIDOTE #1: CLEARLY DEFINE BOUNDARIES

The first antidote is to clearly define the boundaries of your work
schedule. My former executive and I failed to do this, so I would
get pinged about work at all hours of the night, on weekends,
and while on vacation. I rarely had a day off or a vacation with

zero interruptions. Thankfully, I have defined boundaries with my current executive, and it has made a world of difference.

For example, every weekend we go offline for at least twenty-four hours straight. During the week, we typically work evenings on Monday and Wednesday, but not on Tuesday, Thursday, or Friday. This eliminates the daily "Am I going to get some work done this evening?" question. Not to mention, our families know when they'll have our undivided attention, and when we'll be busy. (Note: There are seasons during which we work a couple more evenings and over the weekend. I knew this would happen when I took the job, and I'm OK with the busier seasons because they're the exception, not the rule.)

Once your work schedule is agreed upon, set the expectation that when you're offline, you won't respond unless it's a true emergency.

Speaking of emergencies: Think about the last time your executive sent you a text during off-hours. Could they have waited until you were back online to address the issue? Would a simple email asking you to take care of it the next day have been sufficient? Most likely, the answer is yes.

True emergencies happen, but your executive calling something an "emergency" doesn't make it a true emergency. Most things can wait. After all, "urgent" is rarely urgent, so work with your executive to clarify what is—or isn't—an emergency. Once you've done this, you can make better decisions in those moments of offline panic.

Just as important as setting boundaries is setting yourself up to be able to abide by them. When you're at work, be disciplined and focus on producing so you can go home with a sense of accomplishment instead of feeling like you need to work to catch up.

ANTIDOTE #2: FIND A HOBBY

When I was seventeen, I taught myself to play guitar, and it quickly became a life-giving hobby. I'd lock myself in a room and practice for hours at a time, late into the night. My parents enforced a curfew, but it just motivated me to learn how to play quietly so they wouldn't hear me. Eventually, I got a solid job playing music every weekend for multiple church services, which was a dream come true. After a few years, however, I lost my passion for it. I'd pick up my guitar, but I wouldn't enjoy the music. Instead, I'd stress out about logistics like whether I'd be able to find a drummer that week, or whether our venue was available for a rehearsal.

When I no longer needed to play music to pay the bills, I assumed playing guitar would reclaim its place as my recreational hobby. Unfortunately, that didn't happen. It still felt like work to me, so I couldn't enjoy it like I had before. Then I made a mistake by failing to replace my old hobby. Instead of finding a new hobby that would allow my mind to create and cultivate, I would work on my days off. Unfortunately, I didn't prioritize my enjoyment of life until years later.

These days my hobby is podcasting. I love audio production, interviewing interesting people, and thinking about creative ways to share my show with the world. There will likely come a day when this hobby ceases to be life-giving, and when that day comes, I hope to remember to find a new one ASAP. But until then, I'm enjoying every minute of it.

Spending time on a hobby is one of the most practical and powerful things you can do to resist burnout. If you already have one, block out time to enjoy it on a regular basis. If you don't have a hobby, find something you enjoy doing—something that challenges you intellectually, mentally, spiritually, emotionally, socially, or physically. There are thousands of hobbies in the world, so if you need an idea, start Googling.

The point is to regularly spend time doing something you enjoy, other than work—something that actively stimulates your mind, not something you passively consume. For example, zoning out watching Netflix or Disney+ doesn't count (sorry).

Take a minute to choose one or two hobbies you're going to spend time on in the next couple of weeks. Next, schedule hobby time on your calendar, and if required, order gear or supplies today so you have what you need when the time comes.

ANTIDOTE #3: REDUCE DECISION FATIGUE

As you make more and more choices throughout the day—no matter how big or small they are—your ability to make informed decisions deteriorates. This is known as "decision fatigue." For example, if you spend five minutes in the morning choosing what to eat for breakfast or what shirt to wear, you're using up valuable decision-making energy that you'll need for that big meeting after lunch.

Here are a few tips for reducing decision fatigue:

- Block off five minutes each night to decide what you're going to wear the next day.
- Always schedule important meetings—where big decisions

have to be made—for early in the morning, before you've exhausted your decision muscles.

- Have a running list of your and your executive's favorite orders at restaurants you frequent. This way neither of you need to waste mental energy perusing the menu to decide what to get.
- Plan your daily rhythms so you know when you're going to work out, check email, or read a book. If you don't schedule your activities, you'll have to constantly choose what to tackle next, which can quickly push you to decision fatigue.

In short, if you constantly run out of energy by lunchtime, eliminate some of the decisions you make each morning.

ANTIDOTE #4: REST WELL

Resting well isn't easy for driven Leader Assistants. A day off is seen as uninterrupted time to get caught up on email or finish a project, right? You tell yourself, "I can't slow down; there's too much work to do," which is another way of saying, "The world will cease to operate if I take a day off." It looks ridiculous as I type it out, but I know this excuse too well because I've made it myself.

If you believe you can't survive without working on your days off, you might as well wear a sign on your back that says, "Next Stop: Burnout." I don't care if you're the President of the United States, the Queen of England, or the coolest thing since sliced bread—you need rest. Heck, even God rested on the seventh day, and Jesus took a nap on a boat in the middle of a storm. Of course, I conveniently forgot all this when I thought everything depended on me.

The rest we so desperately need won't happen until we stop

pretending the world revolves around us. Let's make it a priority to give ourselves quality time off on a regular basis to rest and recuperate.

Now, you might rest a bit every week, but when was the last time you took a real vacation? By "real," I mean an extended time away from the office where you didn't check your email or receive a text from your executive.

I went several years without taking a real vacation. I bought into the lie that if I took time off, I was lazy. I even had an executive who, when I returned from vacation, would make subtle, passive-aggressive comments like "We weren't able to do that while you were gone" or "If you would've been here, that wouldn't have happened." Being made to feel guilty about self-care is a surefire sign of a toxic environment—one I didn't see until later, unfortunately.

Since my burnout, I've learned to guard my vacation time. I don't care if you call me lazy, say I'm not hustling enough, or make me feel bad for being offline—I'm taking all of my paid vacation time. I refuse to wait until I'm retired to take a vacation.

I recently received an email from an assistant about to turn sixty. She said the older she gets, the more she realizes how precious time is. She let me know her friend, an assistant for fifty years, passed away last week. That friend had retired just three months before passing. She told me, "You're right not to wait until we retire, because we aren't guaranteed it. We need and must make the most of the time we're given."

Another assistant with twenty-seven years of experience told me she'd always said she'd travel when she retires. Then one day it hit her: why wait? It took a lot of planning, but she took a five-week vacation and hiked five hundred miles across Spain by herself. She didn't check her work email once while she was away, and guess what? The world didn't fall apart. What's more, the experience gave her a whole new perspective on life and made her much stronger emotionally, physically, and spiritually. She just bought her plane tickets to head back to Spain next summer for another three-week hike, and she says she can't wait.

Leaders celebrate, encourage, and even require rest. Take a few minutes to examine your vacation habits, or lack thereof. Do you have regular rhythms of rest built into your schedule? If not, make it happen before burnout creeps in. Being rested is better than being burned out. I know from experience.

Scheduling time off is great, but knowing what to do with that time is just as important. Here are a few practices that help me keep my "off" time from turning into "on" time so I can rest well.

TURN OFF NOTIFICATIONS

Maybe you use your phone to take pictures of your kids or look up BBQ recipes. That's fine, but turn off notifications, rearrange the apps on your home screen, or use the "Do Not Disturb" feature to your advantage. Sign out of your work email and IM accounts, or lock your devices in a safe, if that's what it takes. Eliminate whatever could draw you into work mode.

WRITE DOWN YOUR GOALS

Before you log off for the weekend, think through three or four items you want to accomplish when you get back from your break. Don't over-analyze how you'll accomplish each one. Just quickly list them out in a journal or email them to yourself. This will help you clear your head so you can enjoy the time off.

SLEEP

I know it's cool to brag about your lack of sleep in some circles today, but it's not healthy. Try going to bed early or sleeping in, and don't feel guilty about either one. If you're tired in the middle of the day, take a nap. The best part about sleeping? You can't work while you're asleep. At least, I haven't met anyone who could.

SPEND FOCUSED, ONE-ON-ONE TIME WITH YOUR PARTNER AND KIDS

Go on a walk with your partner. Take each of your kids out for a meal or treat. Play a board game (even if you prefer to call them "bored games" like I do). Watch a movie, then discuss it. Ask your family what they would like to do, then do it with them. And remember: your phone's notifications will be off while you're enjoying your family.

EXERCISE

Like me, you probably stare at a computer all day at your job, so take advantage of every chance you get to move around. Play tennis, go on a hike, do jumping jacks, or go for a swim. You can go for a run, too, but only if something or someone is chasing you.

At work, I take the stairs 99.9 percent of the time. When I'm on phone calls, I pace back and forth in a conference room or go for a walk. I also try to stay active during my free time.

My favorite vacations involve hiking all day in the mountains, especially now that I know to avoid glaciers.

I hope the above practices help you rest well like they've helped me over the past few years.

ANTIDOTE #5: ASK FOR HELP

One of the biggest lessons I've learned in my time as an assistant is this: If you want to lead well without burning out, you need help. Trying to do everything yourself won't get you very far and certainly won't be enjoyable. Whether it's a career coach, life coach, physical trainer, or therapist, every Leader Assistant can benefit greatly from professional help.

I'm also a firm believer in letting your executive know when you're approaching burnout. I know it can be intimidating and make you feel like a failure to admit it, but they need to know where you stand. In fact, if you go back and look at the list of burnout stressors, you'll notice most of them have to do with your work environment. The odds are your executive directly contributes to your health (or lack thereof).

Be a leader by asking your executive to help you apply the antidotes. Being vulnerable and asking for help could be the most potent weapon you have against burnout.

LEAD YOURSELF

You may be on your way to burnout, or already there. Or maybe you're recovering from recent burnout. Wherever you are on the continuum, don't lose hope. Learn to lead yourself by being aware of stressors that could cause you to burn out. Keep an eye out for signs of burnout creep. Have the discipline to establish healthy rhythms to counteract burnout trends in your life.

Remember my journey on Andrews Glacier? It wasn't over once I crossed it.

Our group breathed a big sigh of relief at first, but then my dad saw what was ahead of us: a forty-five-minute climb down dozens of large, wet boulders. He urged us to focus and take each step carefully. One bad step could mean a broken ankle or worse. In other words, we couldn't get comfortable once we conquered Andrews Glacier. There was another challenge in our path.

The same goes for your journey. You might think you're in the clear after crossing a major glacier without burning out. You might have bounced back well from previous burnout. But no matter what, don't sleep on burnout. Recognize the lurking dangers. Be thorough and diligent in exercising self-care, and you'll build a sustainable career as a confident, game-changing Leader Assistant.

CONCLUSION

ASSISTANTS LEAD

I hope this book has been (and will continue to be) an empowering guide in your quest to lead well without burning out.

I thought I'd wrap things up with a thank-you note for all you do as a Leader Assistant. When those around you fail to be grateful, return to this book and read this note to remind yourself that you are crucial to the success of your organization and your executive.

ASSISTANT, YOU ARE A LEADER

To my fellow Leader Assistants,

Thank you for replying to that email. Thank you for picking up lunch, creating that slide deck, and booking that flight—all at the last minute.

Thank you for fixing a typo that would've made your executive look unprofessional. Thank you for taking out the trash and ordering more toilet paper. Thank you for helping that new hire figure out the office printer. Thank you for drafting that proposal while your executive was out sick.

Thank you for being hospitable to billionaires and other VIPs while you wait for your always-late executive to show up. Thank you for asking the janitor how their kids are doing.

Thank you for scheduling meetings, rescheduling meetings, taking notes in meetings, canceling pointless meetings, and getting the best snacks for meetings.

Thank you for proactively managing your executive's calendar so they can spend time on what matters. Thank you for having the courage to say no *for* your executive, and *to* your executive.

Thank you for making an executive decision on your executive's behalf when they ask you for help—and when they don't ask you for help.

Thank you for taking responsibility while others point fingers.

Without you, there's chaos. Without you, your executive's world crumbles, and your organization struggles to fulfill its mission.

You're a go-getter, critical thinker, chaos tamer, idea generator, business partner, and decision-maker. You're the wild card every executive wishes they had.

You are a confident, game-changing Leader Assistant.

Thank you for leading!

Jeremy Burrows
#AssistantsLEAD

RESOURCES

EMAIL UPDATES

Let's keep in touch—get updates on free resources, new blog posts, online courses, live events, or just the occasional encouraging note.

Subscribe to my email list at:
LeaderAssistant.com/SignUp

THE LEADER ASSISTANT PODCAST

Podcasts are a great way to be challenged and inspired while commuting to work, going for a run, or doing the dishes. Tune in weekly for practical and relatable conversations on productivity, leadership development, and everything in between. I interview a variety of amazing guests including executives, assistants, thought leaders, and more.

Listen to the show on your favorite podcast app, or stream it online at:
LeaderAssistant.com/Podcast

LEADER ASSISTANT LIVE EVENTS

I have the privilege of traveling around the world to speak to and train assistants. I'd love to meet you at an event in the future!

Check out my speaking and event schedule at:
LeaderAssistantLive.com

ASSISTANT'S GUIDE ONLINE COURSES

Online education is the future of professional development and training. I've partnered with top instructors and subject-matter experts to provide premium online courses on a variety of relevant topics to help assistants lead well.

Visit the *Assistant's Guide* online training platform at:
AssistantsGuide.com

LEADER ASSISTANT ONLINE COMMUNITY

Connect with, support, and encourage assistants all over the world in our online groups at:
Slack.LeaderAssistant.com + Facebook.LeaderAssistant.com

ACKNOWLEDGMENTS

———

Thank you, Jesus, for being the perfect example of what it means to be a leader, and for giving me grace when I fail to live up to your example. Because of your life, death, and resurrection, I can be steady, confident, and humble—in work and in life.

Meg, thank you for sticking with me during the worst of my burnout. I'm so grateful for your patience and gentleness toward me. I hope to someday lead as well as you lead our boys.

Weston, thank you for making me laugh and for taking care of your brother. Thank you for being so loving toward your mama. You're going to be a leader who brings joy to many, and I'm proud of you.

Silas, thank you for helping me see beauty in the world. Thank you for being so thoughtful and kind to your brother and mama. I'm proud of you and can't wait to see how you change the world.

Dad, thank you for always believing in me, even during the hard times. Thank you for teaching me how to negotiate and fight for what's right.

Mom, thank you for raising me, homeschooling me, and caring for me—even when I was ungrateful. You're the most loyal person I know. Oh, and thank you for the details and organization skills—they've served me well in my career as an assistant!

To my brothers and sister, thanks for putting up with your older brother's shenanigans all these years. Kyle, thanks for showing me it's possible to run your own business, on your own terms, and still make a good living. Jacob, thanks for being interested in what I do and for being a fun uncle for Weston and Silas. Paige, thanks for standing up for what you believe in, and for being such a kind and forgiving sister, even when I don't deserve it.

Justin, thank you for loving my sister well. Melissa, thanks for putting up with Jacob; I'm not sure how you do it.

Bill and Cathy, thanks for your encouragement and support, and for taking Meg and the boys to the beach while I borrowed your office to write this book.

Rob, Cale, Kernal Jay, Sean, Cameron, and Rick, thank you for being there when my world fell apart.

Darrin and Amie, thank you for encouraging me since I was twelve years old. Supporting your family was the most challenging yet rewarding six years of my life. I learned so much from the wins *and* losses during that season of my life, without which, this book would never have been written.

David and Erin, supporting your family has been an enormous blessing. Thank you for giving me the opportunity. I pray we get to work together for many more years.

Mike Weinberg, thanks for being my biggest fan from day one. Your support and feedback have made my business, including this book, much better.

Monique Helstrom, thank you for taking a chance on me by being a guest on my podcast, and then taking another chance by writing the foreword to this book! I'm thankful for your support and our newfound friendship.

Al-Husein Madhany, thanks for your contributions to this book. I've enjoyed our partnership and look forward to many more business ventures in the future. Stay awesome, friend.

Jillian Hufnagel, thank you for allowing me to include your valuable insights. I've learned so much from you and appreciate your support.

John Ruhlin, thank you for telling me about Bonnie Low-Kramen and for rooting for me over the years. Bonnie, thank you for being so supportive and kind to me, a rookie. Thank you, Bryan Miles, for your generosity and support.

Thank you to all the administrative professional advocates who've supported me on my journey: Nicky Christmas, Annie Croner, Maggie Jacobs, Christina Holzhauser, Lucy Brazier, Linda McFarland, Hallie Warner, Melba Duncan, Phoenix Normand, Trish Stadler, Melissa Peoples, Simone White, Diana Brandl, Jess Lindgren, Emily Burley and the ELS team, Hilani Ellis, Gina Cotner, Crystal and Paige from Base, and many more.

Several amazing people reviewed portions of this book to help me make it better. First, thank you, Kyle Woodley, the rockstar copy editor who put this manuscript through the fire, making it exponentially more clear, powerful, and grammatically correct. Thanks to Rob S., James S., Whitney D., Laura L., Kaitlan N., Sonia N., Stephanie D., and Michael C. for giving me helpful feedback as well.

Thank you to the hundreds of Leader Assistants who filled out a feedback survey during the writing process. Your insight helped shape my ideas in ways that made this book more than I ever thought it could be. In fact, the quotes featured across this book's chapters were just a few of the hundreds of great responses I received when I asked you: "What makes an assistant a leader?" Thank you for contributing your ideas. I'm proud to have included your quotes, as opposed to quotes from historical figures, celebrities, presidents, or Nobel Prize winners. Your voice is just as important as anyone's.

Finally, thank you to everyone who has read one of my blog posts, listened to—or been a guest on—one of my podcasts, sent me an encouraging note on LinkedIn, or said hi to me at an event. Helping Leader Assistants all over the world gives me so much joy, and I'm honored to be a small part of your journey. Keep leading well, friends.

ABOUT THE AUTHOR

 **JEREMY BURROWS** is a longtime executive assistant, international speaker and trainer, and host of the No. 1 podcast for assistants: *The Leader Assistant Podcast*. His passion is helping assistants and executives lead well without burning out.

Jeremy has worked with CEOs, professional athletes, Fortune 100 board members, billionaires, pastors—and their assistants—in both the nonprofit and for-profit sectors. He's currently Executive Assistant to the Founder and CEO of Capacity, an artificial intelligence SaaS company.

Jeremy was raised in Kansas City, MO, and is a die-hard fan of the Royals and Chiefs. He loves the mountains, music, and craft beer. He lives in St. Louis, MO, with his wife, Meg, and their two boys, Weston and Silas.

To learn more about Jeremy's training resources for executives and assistants, visit:

GoBurrows.com

Made in the USA
Monee, IL
23 February 2021